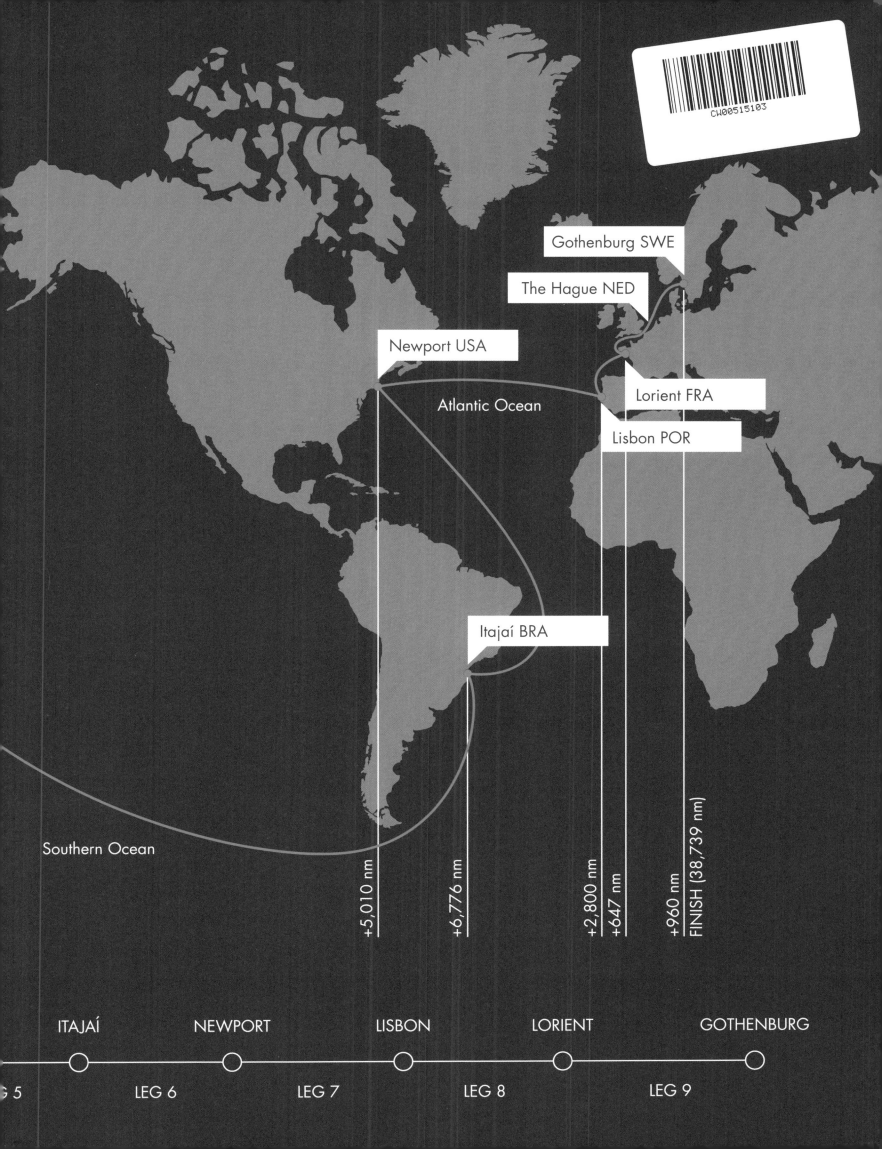

Journey of Change

WOMEN PUSHING BOUNDARIES

To Christine for Crimble 2015 ☺ Respect to all of you Girlies and your enjoyment of life!! love from David e Fiona x xxx

This book is dedicated to Team SCA coach Magnus Olsson, 1949 – 2013

Journey of Change

WOMEN PUSHING BOUNDARIES

ANNA-LENA ELLED
CORINNA HALLORAN

YVONNE GORDON
RICK TOMLINSON

BOKFÖRLAGET MAX STRÖM

Contents

Optimism and trust are most valuable when challenges lay ahead.
Your diversity is your most powerful asset.
Together you stand strong.

H.R.H. Crown Princess Victoria
Godmother Team SCA

This message was inscribed on a
plaque given to the team by Sweden's
H.R.H. Crown Princess Victoria.

The plaque was placed above the galley
on the boat for the crew to see every
day as they raced around the world.

Making Waves

It's 3am off the coast of Lorient, France, and the all-female Team SCA are rounding the tiny Île de Groix. They are 9.6 nautical miles from the finish of the leg. Behind them, Team Vestas Wind and Abu Dhabi Ocean Racing are hot on their heels. Will Team SCA cross the line first, in this Leg 8 of the Volvo Ocean Race? After circumnavigating the globe, and sailing 37,769 nautical miles so far, over nine months, will they beat the six other teams, all male, who they have been leading for three days?

This is Team SCA, the first all-female team to take part in the Volvo Ocean Race in 12 years. There are 11 women on the crew, and all of their sailing, and 18 months of training before that, are falling into place. They have spent hours in the gym and months training on the water, living together, eating together and sailing together, to prepare for this race.

In the race so far, they have been through storms and cyclones, past the icebergs of the Southern Ocean and through the rough South China Sea. They have had injuries, collisions, breakages, broaches, torn sails and Chinese gybes. They've had little sleep, extreme hot and cold temperatures, and freeze-dried food, all while missing family, friends and children. But all the time, they have been learning, about ocean racing, about teamwork, about surviving hundreds of miles from land for weeks at a time and, most of all, about sailing an advanced ocean racing boat as fast as possible. They have beaten the all-male teams twice, in InPort Races, and now they are leading a race leg.

Their coaches, their sponsors and their tens of thousands of fans around the world wait with baited breath as they sail the last miles of the leg towards the Lorient coast. A wrong manoeuvre, strong current, an unlucky breakage or lack of wind could change all the placings, even in these last few miles. But if they win the leg, it could change the future for women in the world's most extreme ocean race.

This is their story…

The Start of the Journey

When SCA announced an all-female team for the Volvo Ocean Race 2014–15 in August 2012, it sent a ripple of excitement through the sailing world. It had been 11 years since a female team had entered the race and women were now back competing in the planet's most extreme offshore sailing challenge.

SCA knew the project would be a challenge – because of the absence of women in the last few editions of the race, it would take a lot of work and commitment to bridge the experience gap and develop a female team which would be competitive at this, the highest level of ocean racing.

A female team made sense for SCA, a Swedish leading global hygiene and forest products company. Some 80 per cent of customers of SCA's products – such as TENA, Tork, Libero, Libresse, Lotus, Tempo and Vinda – are women. The Volvo Ocean Race visits 11 countries over nine months and 38,739 nautical miles, and an SCA ocean racing team would take the company's message and CSR activities around the world, engaging with consumers and inspiring its 44,000 employees worldwide.

It would also form part of SCA's journey of change as a company. Participating in the Volvo Ocean Race would be an important step

in the journey to build the brand and increase awareness of
SCA. It would also reinforce SCA's philosophy of supporting
women's empowerment and helping them to participate fully
in society under the same conditions as men – socially,
educationally and professionally.

To race a Volvo Ocean 65 boat fast around the world, non-stop,
24 hours a day for up to a month at a time, would require the
world's best female sailors, and this meant building and training
a high-performance team who were physically strong, technically
competent and team players.

Since it started as the Whitbread Round the World Race in 1973,
112 women have competed in the race. The first boats in the
race were standard ocean-going yachts, some with chefs, but
now the Volvo Ocean Race is all about speed, performance and
competition, with brutal conditions making it the toughest offshore
race of all. In the race's 42 years, there have only been four all-
female crews and not all have had the same level of backup
and financial support as the male teams. In recent years, women
sailors who wanted to join a team found it nearly impossible, due
to the sheer physical power it takes to sail a Volvo Ocean Race
boat. The new one-design Volvo Ocean 65s for this edition of
the race, although slightly smaller than the Volvo Open 70s of

Left:
Clockwise, from bottom left: Carolijn, Annie, Sam, Liz and Sophie.

"It was the very beginning of the project with the team based in Lanzarote. We were trying to select the core group of crew. We were hoping to get four to seven girls to fill some key areas of the boat. In the end we found five, ticking off some important boxes in terms of crew positions. At this point we understood how big the task ahead was. There was a big gap in experience and knowledge. The VO70 was a good platform to begin the process as it was very similar to the new VO65 that we would be racing."
– Joca Signorini, Team SCA coach

2011–12, are still extremely physically demanding. As well as handling ropes with huge loads, every time the boat changes direction, the crew have to haul up to three tons of kit above and below deck to the other side of the boat – including food, spares and sails weighing 100kg.

Team SCA were aware how male dominated the race was and putting together a female team would mean building experience, in some cases from scratch. Unlike the male teams, who can pick crewmembers who have multiple previous races under their belt (some teams had a combined experience of over 20 Volvo Ocean Races), finding women with such experience would be a challenge. The race's history had also shown that it takes about three races to end up with a place on the winner's podium (top three) – as in any top-level sport, you can't expect to win first time.

With Richard Brisius, who had participated in two previous Volvo Ocean Races and run five successful Volvo Ocean Race campaigns that included two wins with EF Language and Ericsson, on board as managing director of Team SCA, the work started as soon as the 2011–12 race was over. They were first to order a Volvo Ocean 65 and while waiting used the old Puma VO70 – Il Mostro from 2011–12 – for training.

Right:
The crew ate all meals together in Lanzarote. Food was an important element in training – chef Hanna Björkman worked with team doctor Antonio and fitness coach Santiago to make sure the food could deliver the calories and nutrition the sailors would need. In the initial stages of training, some of the girls would be trying to lose fat, while others would be trying to gain it. During the race, sailors burn around 6,400 calories a day, so during the stopovers the focus was on recovery and recharging for the next leg, while on board the focus was to keep energy and calorie intake high.

The team set up base in Puerto Calero, Lanzarote, in the Canary Islands, which would allow training in reliable breeze and sea conditions off the coast of northwest Africa, and they formulated a plan to put together the sailing team of 11 (female teams are allowed three more crewmembers than male teams). Work also started on the marketing and communications plan, including branding, clothing and visual identity – the result being the distinctive magenta and navy team colours.

The first coach to be involved was one of the world's most popular and accomplished offshore sailors, Magnus "Mange" Olsson, who had competed in six Volvo Ocean Races and won one with EF Language in 1997–98. The next coach was Joao "Joca" Signorini, who had represented Brazil at the Olympics and competed in three Volvo Ocean Races, winning in 2009 on Ericsson 4. Brazilian sailor Torben Grael also provided support.

When the team was announced, Team SCA received hundreds of applications for the positions. For the crew, applications came from every area of sailing, from Olympic sailors and world champion match racers to round-the-world solo sailors – women with impressive track records at the highest level of sailing. Of these, around 40 applicants were invited for trials. After interviews

"The sailing conditions in Lanzarote were perfect for testing and trialling, day after day. We probably covered 60 miles per day on a normal day, working on driving and trimming skills, and practising manoeuvres. We set up the base and team with the same approach as other Volvo Ocean Race projects we had been part of before. It involved a lot of time on the water, with the coaches sailing with the girls every day. So we were able to pass on our knowledge in handling the boat, and at the same time it allowed us to look at the girls on trial and work out if they were potential candidates." – Brad Jackson, Team SCA coach

and screening, seven candidates were invited to deliver the training boat from Southampton to Lanzarote in January 2013, with five coaches on board – Magnus and Joca plus Casey Smith, Martin Strömberg and New Zealander Brad Jackson, who had competed in four and won three Volvo Ocean Races and was joining as full-time coach. After a successful trip to Lanzarote, daily training started from the base in February 2013. The first months were about training the crew but also assessing their skills and if they would fit into the team. Various crewmembers were trialled – with three-week periods of sailing, fitness, medical evaluations and interviews – and some were invited back a second time.

In March 2013, five of the seven candidates who sailed from Southampton were signed up to the team: Sam Davies, Carolijn Brouwer, Annie Lush, Sophie Ciszek and Liz Wardley. After early morning gym sessions each day, the team had breakfast together and then sailed from mid-morning to late afternoon, with regular overnight sailing training sessions. After debriefs and dinner, the demanding schedule didn't leave much time for other activities.

As well as being in peak physical fitness, being medically fit was also important. Team doctor Antonio Zoido monitored every aspect of the girls' health, working to find the optimum balance of training, nutrition and resting for performance. Each crewmember

had a full medical, body metrics and VO2 fitness tests, with goals based around fitness and nutrition. Later, Antonio also trained Sophie, Sally and Dee to be paramedics, covering everything from inserting IV catheters to CPR and suturing.

On 23 April 2013, there was a sudden and devastating event which brought Team SCA to a standstill. Magnus Olsson (64) passed away, following a massive stroke a few days earlier. Joined by Magnus's family, the team was shocked and there was a long period of mourning. But the day after Mange had gone, one of the crew members said: "We cannot disappoint Mange now – and we will not." The team vowed to continue the training and preparation work that Magnus was so committed to, knowing he would not have wanted anything else.

They continued training through the summer and in August 2013 competed in the 600-mile Rolex Fastnet Race in their VO70 boat, their first time to race fellow Volvo Ocean Race competitors, Abu Dhabi Ocean Racing, who they beat on corrected time.

In October, more crew were confirmed – Abby Ehler and Stacey Jackson – and the new Volvo Ocean 65 boat arrived, ready for them to sail from the UK to Lanzarote. On board was new coach, Norwegian Aksel Magdahl, a navigation and routing specialist

who had done two previous races. In January 2014, Sally Barkow and Justine Mettraux were confirmed on the team, followed in March by Dee Caffari, Sara Hastreiter and Elodie Mettraux, who joined her sister Justine, making the pair the first sisters to sail together in the race.

In April 2014, the team faced their first big offshore challenge with a transatlantic crossing to Newport, Rhode Island, USA. The trip took 14 days and provided ideal training with all types of wind conditions. In June, meteorologist Libby Greenhalgh joined the team, followed by Onboard Reporters Corinna Halloran and Anna-Lena Elled. After sailing back to Lanzarote, they competed in the Round Canary Islands Race in July 2014.

At the end of July, Team SCA left their training base at Puerto Calero for good and in August 2014 took part in the Sevenstar Round Britain and Ireland Race, along with four other teams – Abu Dhabi Ocean Racing, Team Campos (later to become Mapfre), Team Alvimedica and Dongfeng Race Team. The 1,850-mile race started in the tail end of Hurricane Bertha and Team SCA smashed the world record for a women's monohull to complete the course.

They were now all set for the big challenge, the 38,739-mile Volvo Ocean Race around the planet against six other teams…

Previous pages:
One of the key aspects of the training was fitness. The girls started in the gym at 7am each morning, under a special programme developed by their physical coach and physio, Santiago Casanova, who was fitness coach for the winning Groupama team in 2011–12. As well as daily gym sessions, the team did everything from running, swimming and cycling to high jump, long jump and mini triathlons.

"We couldn't have asked for anything better. Preparing for the Volvo Ocean Race on the fitness side, we had an ideal place for it in Lanzarote. It was 100 per cent customized for our needs. If I was to prepare another team for this race, without a doubt this would be the place of choice."
– Santiago

Below:
The operations team planned the logistics of getting food and containers of equipment for the race around the world and to the 11 stopovers along the way, organizing everything from food to accommodation and transport.

"Lanzarote is an easy choice for a sailing training location. We enjoyed perfect sailing conditions and great local facilities during our 15 months of pre-race training." – Anna Goyne, Team SCA logistics and operations manager

Opposite, top:
"The girls were coming from different backgrounds and had different experience, most of them at quite a high level in what they were doing before, so how to find the limits and to understand the way to race the Volvo boat was new – so that was our focus from the start. From day one we knew they had sailing skills but we were looking to find that small percentage here and there. That's the whole game when you're racing and finding the limits. You're not just trying to helm the boat, it's all about accuracy and small details. These boats are very sensitive to small angles so you can find a big difference in performance between a few degrees here and there." – Joca

Opposite, bottom:
"Driving for the first time was incredible. The speed, the feel, my heart was racing. I turned around to Sam and said 'why have I been racing Ynglings for years when people have been sailing these?' I was sold." – Annie

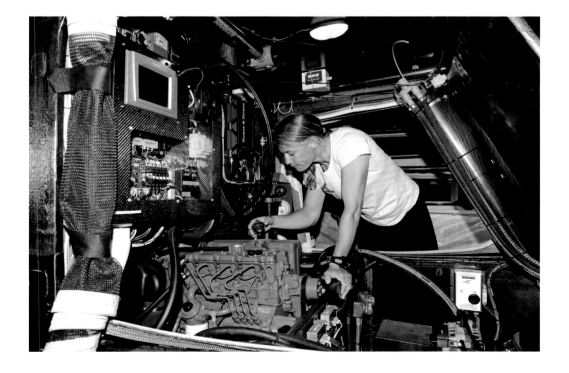

Left:
The Team SCA Volvo
Ocean 65 and the
larger Volvo Open 70
(right), which they used
for training.

"The two-boat testing was
vital to the campaign
because we were able
to bring in more girls
and also more coaches,
between both boats,
and create a racing
atmosphere. The intensity
of having two boats to
race each other is always
an advantage, whether
you are working on the
development of the boat
or on racing skills." – Brad

Opposite, top:
"We were just getting sprayed. The transatlantic was the biggest preparation for Leg 7 of the race. It was the biggest insight into what we were up for!" – Stacey

Opposite, bottom:
"We were arriving back in Lanzarote after the transatlantic. We had some breakages on the way back, but it was a sense of accomplishment because we'd made it across the Atlantic and back. It was the first time we'd completed something like that on our own. Now we knew that we could do any leg of the race. We also learnt a lot about the boat and what it could and could not do in a lot of different conditions." – Sally

Below:
The Team SCA Volvo Open 70 at the start of the Rolex Fastnet Race in 2013, the team's first major race. The team led their class around the iconic Fastnet Rock and finished ahead of Abu Dhabi Ocean Racing on corrected time.

Following pages:
"That moment was during the Round Britain and Ireland Race. I had to get an interview from Sam for Volvo Ocean Race. She picked up the boat camera and started shooting and then turned around to take a selfie. She said the conditions reminded her of being in the Southern Ocean. I never realized at that moment how much traction that image would get." – Corinna

Alicante start

This was the third time the Spanish city had hosted the Volvo Ocean Race start and while the Race Village was only open for the two weeks leading up to the start, most of the teams were on site from early September.

SCA fans in the Race Village

The Skippers Press Conference ahead of the start

Joséphine Edwall-Björklund presents the SCA consumer study for Hygiene Matters

Spectacular view of the race fleet from the balcony of the SCA Pavilion

Thousands of visitors at the Race Village

SCA donated 1,000 saplings to the Alicante region

Annie Lush preparing the food bags for Leg 1

Carolijn shares a moment with son Kyle, before the race start

The SCA Pavilion lit up at night

The seven Volvo Ocean Race skippers. Back row, left to right: Bouwe Bekking (Team Brunel), Charles Caudrelier (Dongfeng Race Team), Charlie Enright (Team Alvimedica) and Ian Walker (Abu Dhabi Ocean Racing). Front row, left to right: Iker Martínez (Mapfre), Sam Davies (Team SCA) and Chris Nicholson (Team Vestas Wind).

Dee takes part in a TENA pelvic floor exercise event

Local children join a fitness class outside the SCA Pavilion

Recording the cover of Avicii's "Wake Me Up" as the team song

Billboards on the Paseo Maritimo

Guests on board for the ProAm Race – guests can join the crew for selected races which don't count for overall points

Johan Sahlström and Anders Gaasedal, creators of the Lego model, showcase their masterpiece for the first time

Sally counts up the food bags ready for the leg to Cape Town

Sophie jumps overboard as part of a practice emergency procedure

Images of the sailing team in the marina

The crew are joined by international guest bloggers for an early morning fitness session on a beach in Alicante

Prince Carl Philip of Sweden gets a chance to helm the Team SCA Volvo Ocean 65, with skipper Sam Davies giving advice

Stacey, Dee and Libby hold mini Lego action figures of themselves. The other mini Lego team members can be seen in the foreground.

Baptism of Fire

Leg 1: Alicante – Cape Town

As dawn broke in Alicante, Spain, on 11 October 2014, the women of Team SCA were getting ready for the biggest challenge of their lives: a 38,739-mile offshore race around the planet. Feeling fit and strong after all their training, there was a mix of excitement and nerves among the crew. The first leg to Cape Town in South Africa – 6,487 nautical miles and the second-longest leg in the race – would be a baptism of fire.

Watched by thousands of spectators, the seven boats in the race and their 66 sailors crossed the start line in warm, light winds. On board the boats, the teams were in full race mode from the start. The first night was full of direction changes and sail changes according to wind-shifts, with little sleep for the crews. On day two, a bold tactical move saw the girls split from the rest of the fleet to sail north through the Strait of Gibraltar while the others stayed south. The position report on 13 October showed that they were 18 nautical miles ahead of the fleet. They were in the lead.

Team SCA was the first boat to escape into the Atlantic

Ocean. On board, the crew settled into their daily rhythm – watch, eat, sleep and repeat – with a four-hours-on, four-hours-off watch system. They also got used to the freeze-dried meals and to the six-hourly position reports, showing the position of all boats in the fleet.

Over the following days, highs included seeing dolphins and sailing close to Mapfre; lows were getting caught in a fishing net and position reports showing they'd slipped to the back of the fleet.

On 24 October, Team SCA celebrated crossing the equator into the southern hemisphere with a traditional visit from "King Neptune". In the doldrums, they experienced everything from thunderstorms and strong winds to agonizing hours of no wind, leaving them miles behind.

As they sailed into the Southern Ocean, temperatures dropped, the water became cooler and sun cream was swapped for fleece hats. Team SCA averaged speeds of 19 knots, surfing

down waves. Despite white water constantly crashing over the boat, the crew sailed full throttle, determined to catch their competitors.

In the final few days, nearing Cape Town, as the crew looked forward to hot showers and fresh food, Team SCA encountered Mapfre running out of wind under Table Mountain. The battle was on for sixth place. After 26 days and 23 hours at sea, Team SCA crossed the finish line in sixth place. Having sailed 8,500* nautical miles, they snuck past Mapfre in the final 10 miles. It was a lesson to never give up. Sara said it was one of the best moments of her whole life.

There were still eight more legs to go…

* Actual miles sailed for each leg are always greater than the estimated leg miles.

Opposite, top:
In the hours after the start, watch captain Liz and navigator Libby (in the background) at the navigation station prepare for the 6,487 miles ahead to Cape Town.

"You go from looking at quite a small area and a short course, to looking at the much longer term, so we're positioning ourselves where we want to be. You've always got to have that bigger picture. Here, Liz is reading through the notes from our shore support on the navigation side, for what's coming up – the next few headlands, the next 12 hours, the next few days – getting herself up to speed as a watch captain of what to expect." – Libby

Opposite, bottom:
Two nights into the race, sailing past Gibraltar, the team gets used to night sailing.

"We're still trimming and working and we're talking about how we're sailing the boat fast, but then you can't see so much and you're relying on the numbers more, on the instruments which are lit. You've got those lights glowing at you, constantly in front of your eyes. Liz is writing some notes, she's got her red head torch on. We use head torches because that's easy and discreet. We use red light as much as possible so as not to damage the helmsman's and the trimmer's night vision."
– Sam

Below:
Libby checks the position report – Team SCA had split from the fleet and sailed north, while the rest of the fleet sailed south.

"We saw reasonably early, maybe 12 hours before, that there could potentially be a split. We didn't really think that there would be. I assumed everyone would go north. We got a position report before we entered the Gibraltar Straits and we said: 'Where is everyone?' We were thinking that we were going to converge – some in front and some behind. The position report came in and we were 18 miles ahead. Holy moly, it was pretty cool!" – Libby

Following pages:
"That's a typical doldrums' sky, it's pretty grey so we're probably under a thunder cloud. Then there's rainy clouds, you can see almost the squall line ahead. We've got all the sails on the bow, half the bags open, sails are spilling out. Everything's ready to go. We've also got ones stacked with the strap, so if something happens in a hurry we're not going to lose them overboard. In the doldrums, things change very quickly." – Sam

"There were sail options one, two, three and four, and it was unclear what was going to happen with the weather, so we had every option ready to go. We were trying to defend from the front as we wanted to hold onto our lead."
– Stacey

41

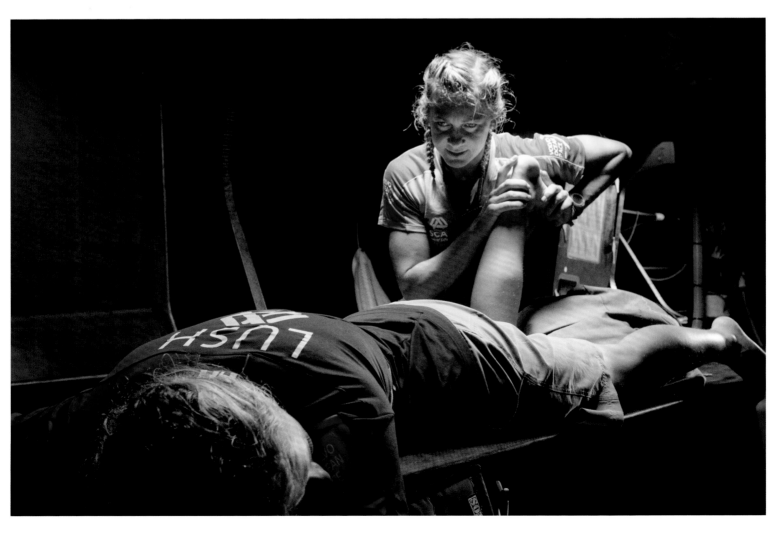

Opposite, top:
"At sunset, the colours are amazing, quite often we're looking for the 'green flash'. I don't think there's going to be one here because there's some cloud in the sky. It's always quite a nice moment to be on watch, sunset watch is always good." – Sam

The team operates on a watch system, with four hours on/four hours off. During the four hours off, the crew have to eat and change, so they often sleep for only two hours at a time. During off-watch, they can also be woken for sail changes, tacks or gybes, when all hands are needed on deck.

Opposite, bottom:
"Sophie is one of our onboard medics. She's trained as a physiotherapist; we're really lucky to have her on board. If something happens to someone, she is totally understanding and not squeamish. Annie had a nagging Achilles tendon, Sophie's treating her here. She has treated the crew with acupuncture occasionally. She keeps an eye on everyone. It's vital for the crew because small niggles just like this one can suddenly flare up and get infected or become really big problems offshore, and people have had to be evacuated from their boats."
– Sam

Below:
"At high noon, shortly after crossing the equator, King Neptune – Abby – came out in all her glory. King Neptune's assistant, Sophie, was in charge of manning the 'fish stew' Neptune had been brewing the last few days. It included decaying flying fish' guts and leftovers. We were all giddy with anticipation. First we had fish-stew facials. Then, the Pollywogs were tasked with initiation performances. Stacey did five burpees, Sara and Libby had to do a commercial, Carolijn and I sang our team song in 'gospel', and Justine and Annie had to act like our coaches. It was incredible."
– Corinna

"For me it was all about a lot of revenge for the most horrible and personal experience of crossing the equator myself. I was initiated by some salty sea dogs so I wanted to return the favour." – Abby

Following pages:
"I was going through the spare food from each day as we were going to be one or two days longer at sea, so I had to ration enough snacks for the remainder of the leg." – Sophie.

Food bags are numbered by day. Each day, the crew have muesli or porridge for breakfast and a hot dish – stew or curry – for lunch and dinner. Meals are freeze-dried and must be rehydrated with water. Each girl also has two energy bars and a chocolate bar, and there are communal bags of dried fruits and trail mix.

"Eating is just as much a part of the job as sailing hard and fast. A sailor wouldn't show up to watch without being properly hydrated and fed." – Corinna

Opposite, top and bottom:
"The waves out here are, as promised, relentless. Over and over again, cold waves crash over the bow, jumping over the cabin top, crashing into the cockpit, and bouncing off winches and sailors before heading back off the boat. Sometimes, when the foam splashes up it reaches five feet in the air. There's water everywhere. Down below, it's cold and wet – acceptable conditions for outside but sometimes a little more challenging to cope with inside. If you can't get warm, it's incredibly challenging to sleep." – Corinna

"It felt like we were finally doing the Volvo Ocean Race, in the conditions we have grown up watching from the legends of the race. We were finally going fast, it was getting cold and very very wet." – Stacey

"I love the Southern Ocean. It's a shame that there isn't more of it in this race. Just the huge waves and the long wave-lengths and the fact that you're miles away from anywhere. I remember when I first went there I was 22 and you always ask: 'What's it like? How big will the waves be? How cold will it be? When will we see an albatross?' I've done it single-handed since. It's funny, now it was the young ones asking me what it would be like, it was a flashback to when I first went." – Sam

Below:
"I've always said that if it was warmer, say 20 degrees Celsius, then everyone would go sailing in the Southern Ocean. It's the best sailing conditions I've ever experienced." – Carolijn

Following pages:
"Abby's hands. You're not always holding onto a string or rope or pulling. That is just from being wet and the humid atmosphere, and grinding. Gloves just keep your hands wetter; you wear gloves on the colder parts of the legs. One of the things that hurts the most is lifting sail bags and stacking the straps on those. For me it's about day four in a leg, where my hands are so painful, I can barely touch anything. Then your hands get tougher and start looking like that. Especially when it rains and you get the fresh water on your hands – that's when it looks the worst. It's quite embarrassing when you come in after a leg and people shake your hands, because that's one thing you can't really hide, your unladylikeness." – Sam

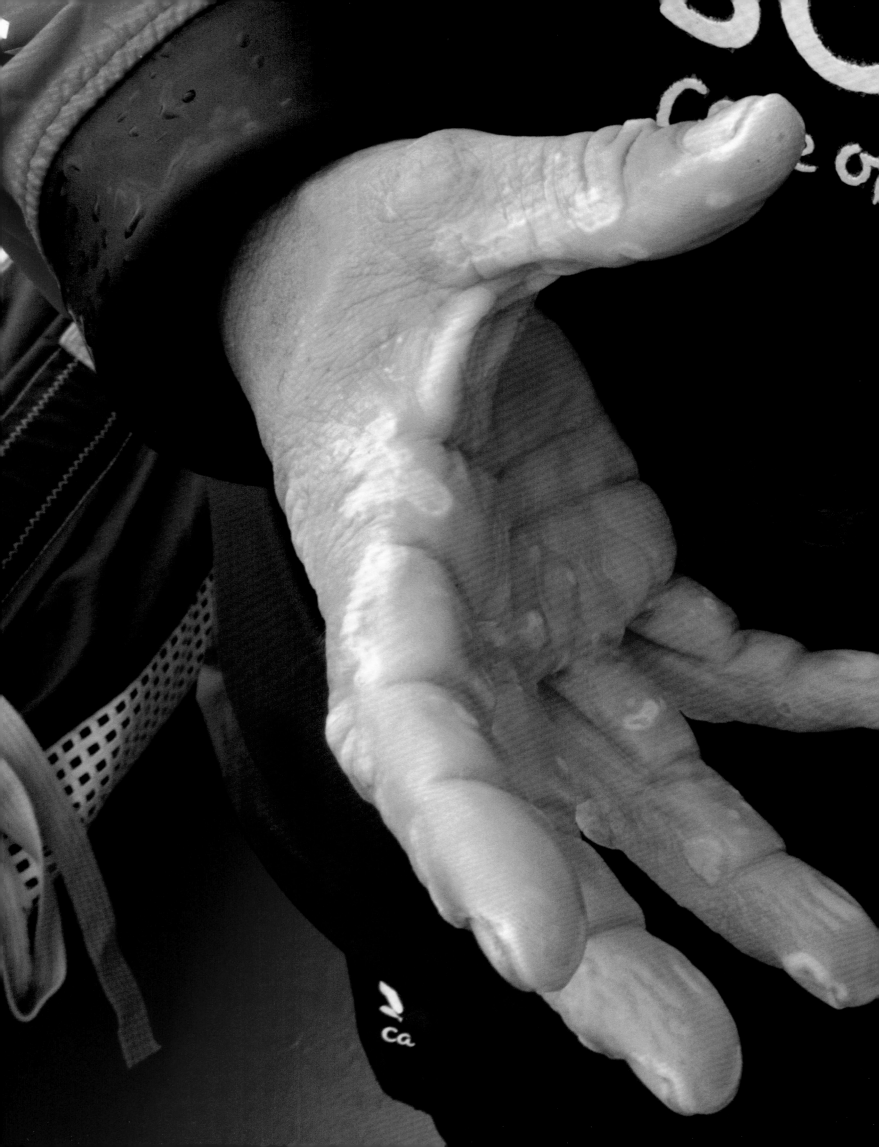

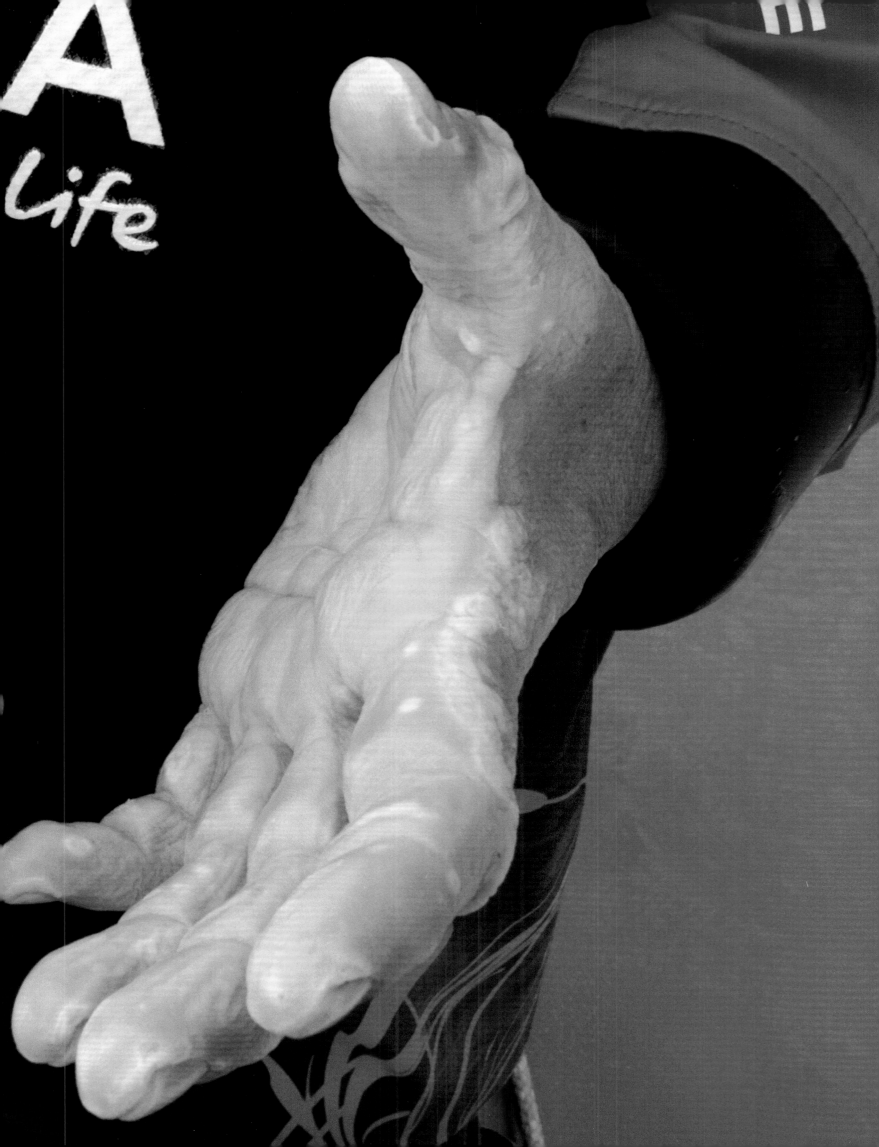

Cape Town stopover

This was the first stopover and a favourite for Team SCA, with friends and family visiting. The crew had opportunities to interact with local CSR initiatives and it was the first time they realized the impact the team was having on a wider non-sailing community.

The crew answer media questions at the Team SCA press conference

Annie meeting staff at Project Playground, an NGO in the Langa Township

Libby takes charge of the champagne moment for the InPort Race celebrations

Stacey on the bow for the Cape Town InPort Race

Team SCA leading the fleet in the Cape Town InPort Race

Guests on board for the ProAm Race pose for a photo with the crew after the race

Mpumi Motsabi, Cuddlers' senior brand manager, at the baby show

The bustling Cape Town waterfront Race Village

Dee with members of the women's sailing team from the Royal Cape Yacht Club

The latest range of diapers being modelled at the Cuddlers' baby show

Sara takes part in a township menstrual hygiene awareness programme

Nontsindiso Tshazi-Kunene, head of sea and rescue in Cape Town

Planting trees at Mseki primary school in Gugulethu

Local township children try on sailor's foul-weather gear on a visit to the SCA Pavilion

Dragon boating competition between the Team SCA sailing team and shore team

Students from a local college after visiting the SCA Pavilion

Fickle Winds

Leg 2: Cape Town – Abu Dhabi

On 15 November, under the shadow of Table Mountain, during an exciting InPort Race with a range of wind conditions, Team SCA secured their first podium position of the race, coming third after a tough battle with Abu Dhabi Ocean Racing and Team Brunel.

After a day of celebrations, the focus soon switched back to offshore racing, and four days later the seven teams started the 6,125-mile leg to Abu Dhabi, in the United Arab Emirates, in strong, gusty winds. After an exciting inshore section, leading positions changed and it was Team SCA that led the fleet out of Cape Town.

As the teams sailed towards the Southern Ocean, the night drew in and the crews readjusted to life offshore. Over the next 24 hours, the weather changed from a warm day with reasonable wind to rough seas, where everything from helming to grinding winches, cooking and even dressing, became difficult. On day three, Team SCA had dropped to 10 miles behind the fleet. As the waves became larger, crews on all the boats battled seasickness and exhaustion.

Opposite:
Team SCA leave Cape Town at the start of Leg 2, under full power.

On day nine, Team SCA became caught in a wind-hole between two areas of low pressure. At the start of the day, Team SCA were 49 nautical miles behind leaders Mapfre – by the end of the day, they were 200 miles behind. As the fleet sailed further away, frustration set in as Team SCA's boat speed was less than one knot. The following day, the tail of a tropical cyclone brought winds of around 22 knots and Team SCA started making up for lost miles.

Suddenly there was shocking news: Team Vestas Wind had run aground.

At sunset on 29 November, Team Vestas Wind ran aground on the Cargados Carajos Shoals in the Indian Ocean. The boat was badly damaged but no one was injured and the crew were rescued. Team SCA, just a few miles behind, were not required to help so continued to catch up with the leaders.

As the wind dropped again, the crew battled strong sun and extreme heat. On 4 December, too far west, Team SCA

gybed north to pick up a wind-shift – which didn't materialize. Over the following days, they lost more miles with every position report. By day 21, they were 460 nautical miles behind the leaders.

Their arrival in Abu Dhabi after 25 days at sea, two days after the leaders, was bittersweet. Happy to be back to shore, they were disappointed at not having been able to truly race the other teams, because of both the weather and mistakes they'd made. But they were determined to learn from any mistakes and show the fleet what they'd got in future legs.

Left:
The boats race in front of Table Mountain, just before the last mark of the inshore section of the start. Team SCA leads Team Brunel, Abu Dhabi Ocean Racing and Dongfeng Race Team.

"It was probably the most memorable race start for me because of the backdrop and the conditions. Before the start, we had 40 knots and we could barely motor out. For me this moment was great as we had a good inshore course that saw us lead the fleet out with Table Mountain in the background." – Sam

Following pages:
Trimmer Annie checks the mainsail, just hours after the start.

"Cape Town was a tough one. The Leg Start was at 6pm local time, whereas all the other starts were at 2pm, so you have another five hours of daylight before it starts getting dark. In Cape Town, two hours out, we were already sailing in the dark. We had to adapt quickly. Here, we're still seeing another boat, Alvimedica, and it is so valuable to be sailing next to another boat and to be able to match or use them as a reference. That obviously is a lot easier during the day rather than during the night." – Carolijn

Previous pages:
"That's a proper squall. There's a fair bit of heel on the boat. And we have reef in as well. We're all trying to have a freshwater shower! There's been lots of changes because you can see rope all over the cockpit floor. Everyone's making the most of the situation to have a freshwater rinse."
– Carolijn

Above:
"We're changing from the J1 to the FRO [Fractional Code Zero] here. This is when we had that six hours of FRO in the Gulf. We had six hours of just sending it, and it was pretty cool. I was up on the bow because Sophie was man down. It wasn't really heavy weather but we had six hours of it – it was just the perfect angle for that sail." – Liz

Right:
"A drowned cat! We went through one really big section of rain and then it calmed down a bit and we pulled the reef out and then we got hammered again. I think it had been an hour and half by the time we settled down fully. I was pretty cold and pretty keen to get off the helm. You can see my hands have gone all white. You don't really realize you're cold until it's over." – Liz

Below and opposite:
On 29 November, Team Vestas Wind ran aground on the Cargados Carajos Shoals (St Brandon), 260 miles north of Mauritius, in the Indian Ocean. Both rudders were broken in the collision, and the stern was taking on water, but – miraculously – no one was injured. For several hours, the crew stayed on board their stricken vessel. The stern was being beaten by the waves as it was stuck fast in the reef. At around 3am, the sailors abandoned the boat and waded through the sea to a dry spot on the reef from where they were rescued by a coastguard boat and taken to the tiny islet of Île du Sud. Team Alvimedica diverted to assist if necessary but were eventually cleared to continue racing north (and later given redress).

Team SCA also offered assistance but were not required.

"It was just pure shock. Sam came on deck immediately when she heard, to inform us about what had happened and none of us could believe it. I was in pure disbelief. We were just relieved that no one was injured."
– Stacey

Previous pages:
"Dolphins just love playing with the boat. They're quite curious. They like hanging around the bow of the boat; they use it as a toy. For us, out there they're just our friends. They come and say hello occasionally. Dolphins are amazing animals and it's nice if you've been sailing around on the ocean and you haven't seen any wildlife, or anyone or any other boat for a week, to have 30 to 50 dolphins come and play with your boat. I guess it's almost a normal thing out there but it does still put smile on everyone's faces." – Carolijn

Opposite and above:
"In the last part of the trip, we saw so many things in such a short space of time, as we turned the corner to see a sea of cargo ships. It was amazing to see land for the first time after 18 days at sea. We were disappointed that we weren't seeing the others, who finished close together, but I remember the lights being so beautiful. Much of what we experienced in this leg was flat water and the 'magic carpet' with all the phosphorus in the sea lighting it up. We had dolphins all around us and often we would literally be sleeping under the stars. It was a really amazing leg." – Elodie

Abu Dhabi stopover

With Christmas and New Year the focal point of the stopover in the UAE capital, most of the crew celebrated with family and friends, and the team also celebrated their first InPort Race win.

Carolijn helming in the Abu Dhabi Practice Race

Camels on the beach in the Race Village

Local stopover staff sporting team colours for the boat arrival

A group of postgraduate aviation students being shown around the boatyard by Felix Schliebitz of the shore crew

The Volvo Ocean 65 gets lifted out of the water for the maintenance period

Sam Davies holds up the InPort Race trophy

The Volvo Ocean 65 fleet crosses the start line

Local Arabian group leads the Sailors Parade

Winners of the female optimist class with some of the SCA crew

Team SCA sails prepared for repair in The Boatyard sail loft

Getting ready for a manoeuvre during the InPort Race

Crew take part in early morning stretch exercises

Sam rides a camel through the Sailors Parade before the Leg 3 start

Liz racing on a traditional dhow boat

The crew visiting the desert, known in Arabic as the Rub' al Khali, or Empty Quarter, which covers 250,000 square miles

The famous Sheikh Zayed Grand Mosque at sunrise

Gybe-Ho!

Leg 3: Abu Dhabi – Sanya

After two tough introductory legs, Team SCA scored their first Volvo Ocean Race victory with a win in the Abu Dhabi InPort Race. In the light, hot airs, an early tack to the starboard side of the course saw Team SCA leave the rest of the fleet behind – they were confident after a win in the Practice Race just days before.

This put Team SCA third in the InPort Race series, a morale-booster before the start of the 4,600-mile leg to Sanya, China. After New Year celebrations, the fleet sailed again on 3 January – minus Team Vestas Wind. The route would take the race around the south of India and through the narrow Strait of Malacca, between Malaysia and the island of Sumatra in Indonesia, the main shipping channel between the Indian Ocean and the Pacific Ocean. They would then turn north along the Vietnam coast and into Sanya on the island of Hainan, China.

In thick fog, the fleet sailed out through the narrow Strait of Hormuz from the Persian Gulf to the Arabian Sea with a night of tacking, avoiding oil rigs and other shipping hazards. On day four, Team SCA were in first position after a gybe but Dongfeng Race Team soon had a grasp on the lead.

Opposite:
"It's rare to see every sunset and every sunrise for many days in a row. Each sunrise experienced on deck is magical, it's as if a great weight has been lifted and a new lease of life injected into the sleep-deprived crew. The orange glow of the lit compass numbers slowly fades and as the dark, muddling veil of night vanishes, suddenly everything becomes easier. In contrast, sunsets have a calming influence on board. Red slithers of sunrays cast across the sky, lighting small wispy clouds and turning the sea gold. If you were to paint these scenes or take a photo, people would think you'd altered them, but it does exist and it's enchanting. That's why, as the sun sets each day, even on our toughest days, there is a sense of euphoria on deck. Out here in the middle of the ocean we're experiencing something very few humans have the chance to. We're the lucky ones." – Annie

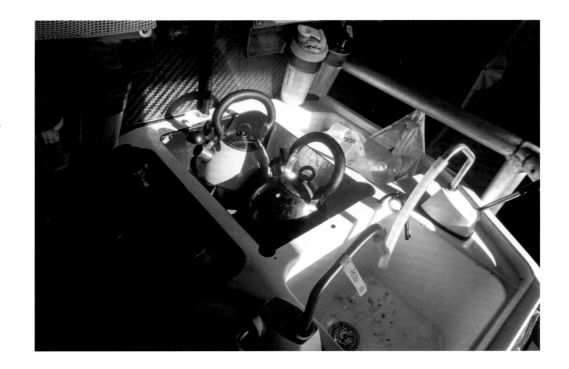

In light, fickle winds Team SCA were racing in the pack, and for the first time they could see the other boats – observing sail changes and gybes for real instead of having to wait for numbers on a screen. One boat they were neck and neck with was Mapfre – with Libby's brother Robert on board.

On day five, the team had a choice of routes to Sri Lanka – to either sail towards the southern tip of India and its sea breezes, or stay offshore to the west. They opted to stay with the main pack. Mapfre gybed and Team SCA saw an opportunity to gain miles, so also gybed. The position report showed none of the rest of the fleet had gybed, so SCA gybed back to its original course. Mapfre followed suit. As Mapfre made small gains with some nicely timed gybes on shifts, Team SCA chose the same strategy, doing 29 gybes over seven hours. The payoff was positive as they had kept in touch with the fleet.

On day 14, Team SCA had a series of events – dodging thunderstorms and enjoying fast sailing – until that evening in the darkness, sailing downwind in strong wind, the Masthead Zero

Left:
"We had a rain squall
and ended up tacking
with the Masthead Zero
on. It did get eased but it
managed to blow around
the daggerboard and put
a cut-out in the shape of
the daggerboard in it. It
was a long process – we
dropped the sail on to the
deck and shoved it down
the front hatch. I put little
bits of repair tape on the
sail, to make it one piece
again, and checked it was
all the right shape. Then
we put on strong, proper
repair cloth. From tearing
it to having it back up took
six hours. With three or
four metres of tear, that's
a good turnaround. When
the hole is big enough for
me to walk through, it's a
pretty big repair." – Stacey

sail suffered damage during a big wind-shift and had a large tear.
Stacey spent hours repairing the sail and it was a team effort to
get it back up quickly and into place. The next day, they reached
the top of Sumatra and started their journey through the busy Strait
of Malacca, avoiding everything from cargo ships and fishing
boats to shallow waters. Another hazard to deal with was floating
objects of all types, from shoes and sticks to plastic bottles and
large floating pieces of wood. Debris regularly had to be cleared
from the keel and rudders.

The next milestone was the South China Sea – described by the
crew as "gravity defying" as they hurtled down waves. They then
tacked up the Vietnam coast, admiring blood-red sunrises as they
dodged hundreds of local fishing boats.

When Team SCA finished in Sanya, after 24 days at sea, the
mood was good. They had been with the fleet for longer, had
improved boat speed and finished within the same 24 hours as
the rest of the fleet.

Previous pages:
"We were quite close to Mapfre for a long time, behind the group, and we saw an opportunity to gain on the shifts, which resulted in a gybing duel with them. It was a whole night of gybing – we did 29 gybes – and at the end we were still with them and had made some gains on the group. At times we'd be getting back in our bunks and it would be as soon as three or four minutes, we were getting called back on deck to do the next gybe."
– Sally

Right:
"Everyone wants to come and have a look at the pink boat with the girls on it. It did create a lot of interest. There was a lot of traffic on this leg. You could tell where we were in the world from what the boats were doing. When we were leaving Abu Dhabi, everyone was taking photos. Later when we get to Vietnam, they're just happy to see people and they're waving. Piracy was in the back of our minds. We'd had briefings about it. We'd been told it was fairly safe now, where we were going. Our biggest fear was running into what the boats might have been attached to at the other end, like fishing nets. That made us more nervous than anything."
– Stacey

Left:
"Part of the challenge of
this race is being able
to fix any part of the
boat should things break
or go wrong. There is
no 'pit lane' to pull into.
Therefore, most of the
crew have secondary skills
ranging from sailmaking to
hydraulic engineering and
boatbuilding to rigging.
This night, Sara and I were
working on one of the
primary winches which
had sheared a split pin
during a manoeuvre."
– Abby

Below:
"We find this situation a lot
on the boat, Libby being
navigator and Sam being
skipper, and I am watch
leader; these two are
constantly discussing the
weather and I am trying
to keep up. When Sam
does a watch handover,
we are probably looking
at where we want to
position ourselves against
Mapfre to do this long
port tack across, which

we would be on for days.
And also when we're in
this situation, they often
use myself or Sally for
fleet positioning. Libby will
explain to us where she
wants to be in regards
to a weather system, but
she'll ask for our advice
on which side of the fleet
we'd like to be. In this
case we were discussing
the fleet but probably
mostly discussing Mapfre
because they were closest
to us."– Carolijn

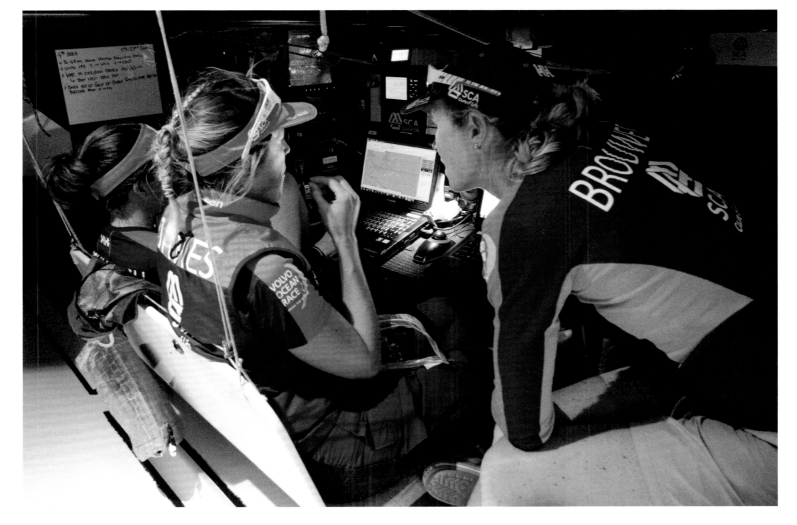

Right:
Clockwise, from far right: Elodie, Sam, Sara and Libby.

"This is the hard thing about light winds. It's frustrating down below too. It got hotter and hotter this leg. You have this 65-foot boat and we're all operating in five foot of it basically. You've got people sleeping. If this was a watch change there'd be some people behind them eating, the Onboard Reporter working. The heads [toilet] are up here as well. It's pretty uncomfortable, the stack of sails, all the people and everything you're trying to do. You're all trying to operate in this tiny, very hot zone. It's pretty hard, there's definitely no space to yourself." – Annie

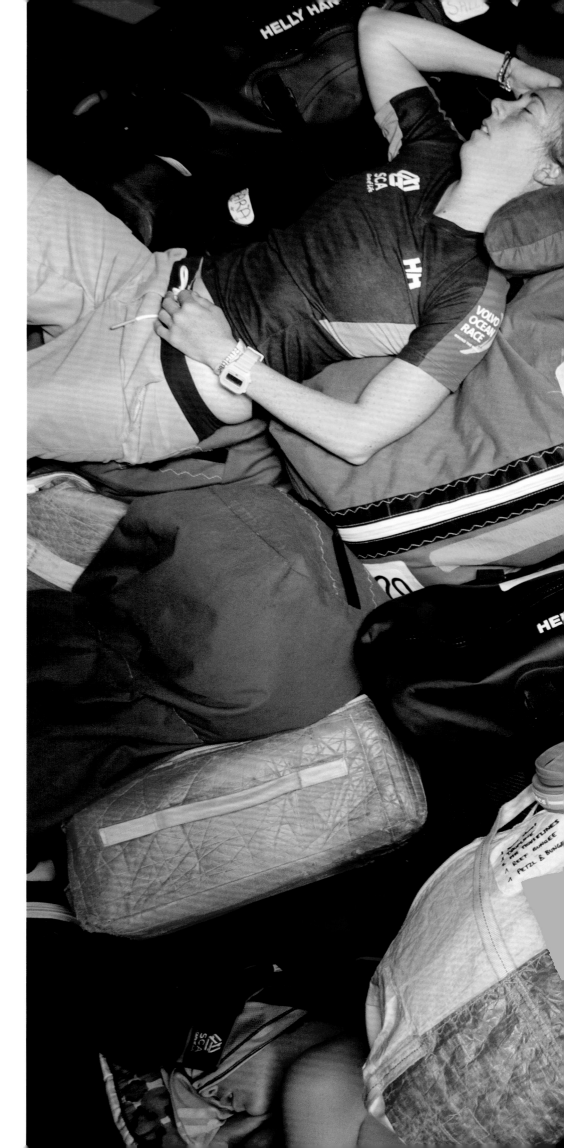

Right:
"This is one of those moments I just hate – bringing the leeward runner forward. We've a reef in the mainsail so it's 20 knots-plus. The boat is at an angle of 25 degrees, and it is one of those high-risk manoeuvres you try not to do too often. You're trying to hold on to the leeward runner, which has a bit of windage on it. With a bit of luck you don't get that wave. At that point I am just hanging on to the vang but later, if I am bringing it forward, once I get to the mast I clip on with my harness, just to take one element out of it – having to hold on, all the fear. It's just another one of those jobs." – Stacey

Following pages:
Team SCA gets one of the biggest crowds of the day as they arrive into Sanya around 8pm.

"We were excited to be arriving somewhere new. It was crazy. It was endless fireworks and there were guys in dragon suits dancing around. It was all quite different – a bit of a surprise when you've just been out there by yourselves for a long time. We were really impressed by the number of people in the crowd. It added to our mood; we were already quite excited. It was a really good arrival. We arrived the same day as the others so we were going to get to have a beer with all the guys. That was the first time we were able to do that." – Annie

Sanya stopover

Team SCA were able to get a taste of Chinese life in this popular tourist resort. However, with a relatively short stopover, the team's focus was on rest and repair to ensure that they were ready for the arduous Pacific Ocean leg ahead.

Team SCA race in the InPort Series

Olympic gold medallist in 2012 Xu Lijia (Lily) with a journalist and his daughter

The public enjoy posing for photos "wearing" the SCA tissue "wedding dress"

The SCA boat's photo-opportunity wall at the SCA Pavilion

The crew walk through the Sailors Parade before the Leg Start

Xu Lijia jumps off the back of Team SCA for the Leg Start

A guest event in the SCA Pavilion

Guests and media on board for the ProAm racing

Team SCA practise the art of Tai Chi

Anna-Lena Elled challenges Jan-Ove ("J-O") Waldner to a game of table tennis

Guests are awarded medals after taking first place in the ProAm racing

Xu Zhengling, deputy mayor of Sanya, visiting the SCA Pavilion

Bertrand Furno, France's consul general in Guangzhou, China, visiting the SCA Pavilion

Girls in Haikou taking part in menstrual hygiene awareness training

SCA's Ulf Söderström speaks at the Team SCA press conference

Nursery children visit the SCA Pavilion

SCA flags and balloons line the Race Village at the Sailors Parade

A Battle
into the Wind

Leg 4: Sanya – Auckland

On 8 February, the giant Guan Yin statue watched over
the fleet of six boats as they started the fourth leg
of the race, leaving behind Sanya for the 5,264-mile
journey to Auckland, New Zealand. In strong upwind
conditions, rough seas and thunderstorms, the fleet sailed
northwest into the South China Sea. All of the teams
described the conditions as the toughest of the race to
date – with big seas causing seasickness and Sam reporting
that extreme heel angles made it difficult to do every task
on board.

On day three, Team SCA and Team Brunel made an early
split from the rest of the fleet, tacking away from the direction
of Auckland, to sail north up the coast of Taiwan, hoping
for more wind later to take them east to New Zealand. The
two boats had a close battle, until a broken halyard lock on
Team SCA saw the J1 sail drop swiftly onto the deck. The J2
went up quickly and an evening repair was prompt, however
Team SCA lost miles to their closest rival.

Over the following days, Team SCA enjoyed big winds,

Opposite:
Justine and Liz on the bow.

*"This is the act of deploying
our outriggers, two-metre
long carbon tubes that
we stick out to leeward
attached to the sheets to
help the trimming of the sail
while heeling over at stupid
angles. You attach all your
anchor points and then
deploy and hope for the
best while you get tension
on everything and then you
step away. If you don't get
hammered by a wave, get
smashed in the face by the
pole or actually lose the
whole lot overboard, you
are having a good day."*
– Liz

waves, sunshine and surfing conditions, with a treat for the girls on Valentine's Day, 14 February – a bundle of cards to open, including some mystery cards from admirers on the other boats!

By day 12, winds had eased and things on board the boat started to dry out. Team SCA sailed south, rejoining the pack as they all sailed in the direction of the Solomon Islands, and delighted to see the outline of both Mapfre and Dongfeng Race Team's sails on the horizon. The next milestone for the fleet was crossing once again into the southern hemisphere, and re-entering the doldrums.

As the crew of Team SCA all gathered on deck to cross the equator, King Neptune made a return visit to initiate Leg 4's Onboard Reporter Anna-Lena on her first equator crossing. Conditions in the transition zone from the doldrums varied in wind strength, with frequent rain squalls as the team kept all sails ready for every wind mode. Light winds and extreme heat followed, as they finally escaped the doldrums and headed for New Zealand.

With Team Brunel still in sight, just five miles away, the focus was on closing the gap, as the crew enjoyed stable winds during the last sprint towards the finish.

Incredibly, after more than 20 days at sea, there was just eight minutes between the first three boats finishing Leg 4 (Mapre, Abu Dhabi Ocean Racing and Dongfeng Race Team), making it the closest leg in the history of the Volvo Ocean Race. Team SCA finished just seven hours behind the leaders, in sixth place.

Previous pages:
"Despite the tough lifestyle, racing continues at 100 per cent all the time on Team SCA. On my last watch we just did the most horrible of all the sail changes you have to do: the J1 to J2 change, a really hard job requiring the whole team on the bow to wrestle the J1 down into its bag and off the foredeck. Life in the washing machine for the girls, and Liz and Stacey did a great job organizing the change and it went really well. We were happy to see that our change was better than that of Alvimedica next to us!"
– Sam

Below:
"This is Liz on the bow, going towards the doldrums. It was hot and sweaty on deck and below deck. As soon as it goes light, the stack internally is moved, people from their bunks moved. It's probably more comfortable to be on deck than below. Although you're exposed to direct sunlight on deck, there's no air down below, that's the hard bit. As soon as you start sleeping in the bow, you're sleeping

close to people, there are no fans or anything. It's amazing what a little fan does in the bunk to cool you down. In the bow you're surrounded by more black carbon and more people."
– Dee

Opposite:
"I had been very sick for the first four days, and this shower made me feel like a new person. It was calm and warm and I took the chance to freshen up while I could. This opportunity doesn't come often on board!" – Elodie

Following pages:
"As we're sailing on an upwind course, the boat is very heeled over, meaning not only are we slamming up and down in the chop but we're also living at 25–30 degrees of heel. Life at 25 degrees of heel whilst pitching up and down is pretty hard, comical at times but mainly just unpleasant. I'm one of the lucky ones and as yet have not felt seasick. Even the toughest and most experienced sailors can get seasick. I think there are probably some conditions the human body just isn't quite equipped to deal with." – Annie

Auckland stopover

One of the race's most legendary stopovers and another family favourite with friends and relatives visiting from far and wide. The crew spent time with previous female race competitors and young female sailors. They also won their second InPort Race.

Women from the Auckland Women in Business Group visit the team base

Team SCA join a tree-planting conservation initiative at Motuihe Island

Previous female race participants enjoy being part of the action in Auckland

Team SCA lead the fleet and win the InPort Race in Auckland

Team SCA with the wreath for Magnus Olsson to be placed in the water at Cape Horn, one of Magnus's favourite places

Images from the winning Team SCA Academy competition photographers on display at the SCA Pavilion

Sara-Jane Blake and the Team SCA crew show off the iconic red socks, symbolic of Sarah's late father Peter Blake and the Sir Peter Blake Trust

Young sailors from Murrays Bay Sailing Club attend a presentation and Q&A with some of the crew

Carolijn, her son Kyle and partner Darren, with other runners, take part in the Round the Bays fun run on International Women's Day in Auckland

Team SCA celebrate winning the Auckland InPort Race

Team SCA fans cheer on the team at the public prize-giving event

Down But Not Out

Leg 5: Auckland – Itajaí

Team SCA ruled the fleet during the InPort Race in Auckland, New Zealand, leading the race from start to finish and becoming the first team to win two InPort Races. This boosted morale in the team as they faced into Leg 5. The longest leg of the race, at 6,776 nautical miles to Brazil, this was also expected to be the toughest. During the previous 2011–12 race, damage sustained in the Southern Ocean forced five of the six boats in the fleet to stop for repairs.

This time, the drama started before the leg even began with a three-day delay to the start due to Cyclone Pam. When they finally got going, the fleet sailed straight into big seas and by day three, they were already in the Southern Ocean and sailing around the ice limit – an exclusion zone which stops the fleet entering an area of icebergs. Annie was nursing a back injury, having been thrown across the boat. By day six, the sailing was fast, skies were blue and survival suits were coming out in the big waves.

On day seven, Team SCA had a few small broaches and were then hit by a squall and pressed down on one side in a Chinese gybe, seriously damaging the FRO and mainsail

Right:
"Once we got down south, the albatrosses were everywhere. They fly effortlessly with their huge wingspan, gliding across the waves. I was comparing my arms to their wings and admiring how amazing they look."
– Sophie

battens. They spent the following days sorting out the mess and making repairs. They sailed on, speeds hampered by the lack of the FRO, a key sail for the Southern Ocean conditions. Elsewhere in the fleet, both Dongfeng Race Team and Mapre also had Chinese gybes. On 30 March, Dongfeng Race Team broke their mast, pulling in to Ushuaia in Argentina and eventually retiring from the leg.

On day 14, a squall of 43 knots took out Team SCA's electrics and instruments, but after much head-scratching and numerous attempts, they managed to repair them. Conditions were cold and hail was falling. They enjoyed more days of fast sailing and bright skies, and on 1 April they rounded Cape Horn, paying tribute to their late coach Magnus Olsson by floating a wreath containing hundreds of messages in the water.

Turning the corner into the South Atlantic, with up to 50 knots of wind, they were now some 580 nautical miles behind the other four boats and suffering without the FRO sail. As Libby reported, just when Team SCA thought the steep learning curve they were on was declining, it had ramped up another level.

Left:
"A big rain cloud came through, and by the time it hit the deck it had frozen. The conditions were pretty moderate and everything was under control so a snowball fight commenced!" – Stacey

Following pages:
"Southern Ocean conditions are attune to being on an extreme roller coaster ride in cold and wet conditions. The acceleration as you surf down waves is exhilarating – and sometimes frightening, as there is no brake pedal to depress when things start to feel on the edge of control. At night the feeling is only exaggerated, as you are unable to see the size or the shape of the waves. Here, deep south, at about 47 degrees south, conditions were cold, rough and wet – about 10 degrees air temperature and 7 degrees water temperature." – Abby

On 5 April, Team SCA hit an object at 22 knots, which knocked the port rudder out of its bearings and damaged the steering arm, sending the boat into a broach. They managed to repair it with a part from the emergency steering. On 6 April, another unlucky collision again damaged the port rudder and caused a broach, losing the team hours.

Team SCA limped into Itajaí on 7 April, broken and exhausted, two days behind the leader Abu Dhabi Ocean Racing, having sailed 7,462 nautical miles and spent 20 days and 17 hours at sea.

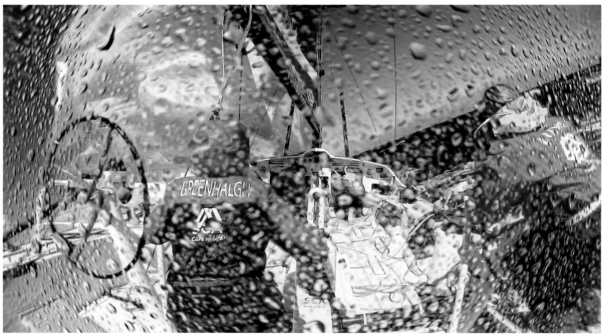

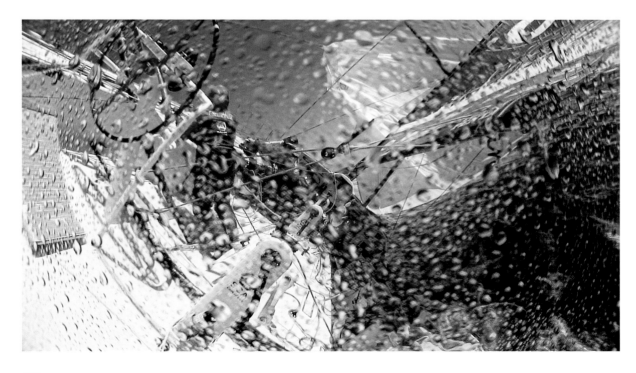

Opposite and below: "One of the worst things that can happen at sea is to Chinese gybe. We had two occurrences of this on Leg 5. The second, less serious one, was as a result of hitting an unidentified object and losing our steering gear. It was daylight and we recovered without any major damage.

"The first one was in the middle of the night and pitch black. We were sailing under the FRO at a fast reaching angle, and quite a big sea running. We just were a bit hot, which is when we got too much pressure on the helm, a little bit too high on the wind angle and you start to lose control of the boat and it wipes out and turn to windward.

"That's basically what started the chain of events. We had a wipe out. It took us a little time to recover, we eased the front sail and it was flapping a lot, and as a result the sail exploded. We lost it from the head to furl, in a straight line down the luff. It was just gone and the whole sail was in the water, acting as an anchor.

"The boat becomes really hard to steer – we went into a Chinese gybe. The problem with that is that everything is on the wrong side weight wise, so your stack, sail stack, internal stack, keel and the water ballast are to leeward and pulling the boat under. When the boat is so over heeled, you can't operate it. You have to climb a mountain to find the rope to ease the sails. It took us a while, it's a far from ideal situation.

"I was on deck but down below it's equally hard to hold on, trying to avoid everything falling.

Eventually we got the boat back under control, the keel to the centre to bring the boat back to horizontal, and we worked on getting the sail back on board. All in all, a fairly costly affair.

"I certainly didn't have any feeling of fear at the time. I think you automatically go into a chain of actions that need to happen, and what needs to happen first, and adrenalin kicks in, but I have never been on a boat that far heeled and I remember I was actually hanging from a piece of rope from a winch – I was standing on the middle pedestal thinking there is no way I could physically pull myself up.

"What would have happened if the boat kept going over? There was just no way it was going to do that." – Abby

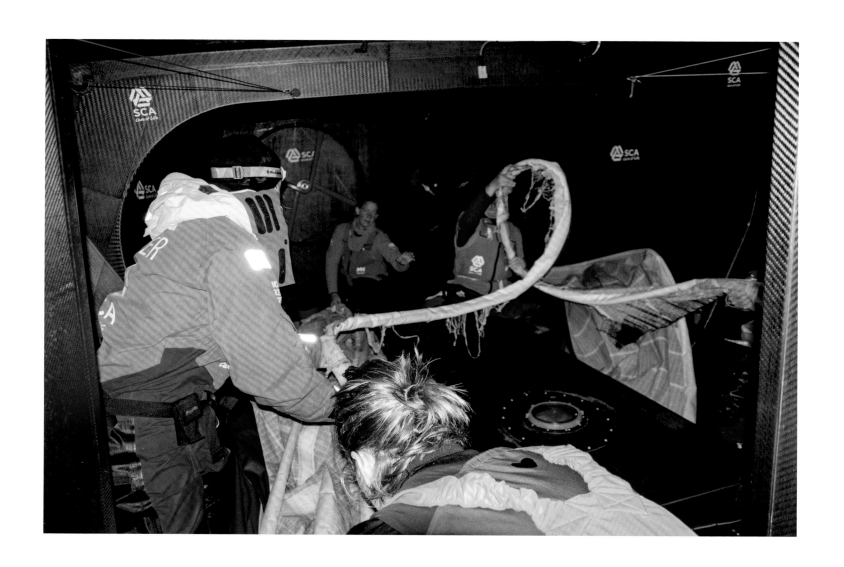

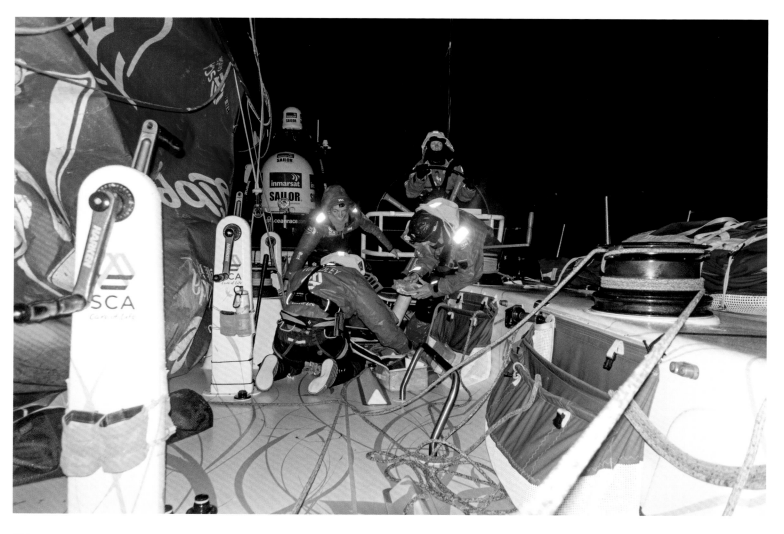

Right:
Abby eats from a dog bowl the crew use for meals to avoid food being spilled.

"As endurance athletes, food is our fuel. It is therefore vital to eat correctly to ensure we function at our best. In the year leading up to the start of the race, our team doctor monitored our body metrics and diet, enabling him to put together our race nutrition, which includes freeze-dried meals, snacks and liquid intake. We have made minor adjustments along the way, as some foods became monotonous, but overall meal plans have been very successful, allowing the team to sustain performance in such an extreme race."
– Abby

"To win you have to finish. Donfeng's dismasting was another reminder that we are not invincible and although it is a race, we must take care of our boat and crew – you have to know when to ease off and when you can push hard. In the Southern Ocean, we are too far away from land to be rescued if something happens. We were glad to hear that they were all okay and that they had a chance to make it to Itajaí in time to be able to restart Leg 6." – Sam

Below:
After 14 days at sea, mostly battling through the Southern Ocean, the first four boats rounded Cape Horn at the tip of South America within an incredible one hour and 18 minutes of each other, with just 15 minutes separating the leaders Team Alvimedica from the eventual leg winners Abu Dhabi Ocean Racing,

who had set a speed record the day before by covering 550.8 miles in 24 hours. Each team reported huge elation after the milestone of rounding Cape Horn, in ideal sailing conditions of northwest winds of 30 knots and a relatively flat sea state.

Following pages:
"An epic moment. Before leaving Auckland, there was talk of a helicopter meeting us at Cape Horn to take photographs of us rounding this iconic cape. When Libby stated the 15-minute countdown to the Horn, I thought she was announcing it as an informative option of a landmark to see – it was blowing 30 knots outside and freezing cold, and I was in a relatively warm, comfortable spot in my bunk. But with Libby's persisting voice as an alarm, it was very clear we were all meant to get up, drag on our wet and cold gear, and get on deck for celebrations. It was freezing and it was amazingly beautiful. The Cape was a monstrous looming rock that visually fulfilled every fantasy of that moment. I was told that was the moment we moved from offshore sailors to offshore legends." – Sara

Left:
"Today has been one of those days when the most simple things in life are challenging. Like walking from one point to another, putting your jacket on, or mixing your porridge without leaving half of the goodies on the floor. The boat has been rocking. It has slammed the waves hard and if you're not holding on to something, the risk of getting airborne and thrown up into the ceiling or launched into the nearest wall is obvious. I was pretty proud, managing to cook both lunch and dinner, neither burning me nor someone in the crew. Add on a fire hose and seawater and you get a pretty good picture of how life is on deck." – Anna-Lena

Right:
"Just being on board is tiring. Nothing is easy. But it is hilarious if you have the power to appreciate it – and spectacular. We are slowly noticing we are getting closer to civilization. We have plenty of birds following us, and just today we've seen two or three ships. It looked like they did struggle quite a bit as well in the rough sea state. One container ship looked like it time after time was being launched from the waves. And I think they were landing hard on the water."
– Anna-Lena

Following pages:
Team SCA arrive in Brazil after 21 days at sea.

"We have a few hours to go, we are very excited to be getting there, and we hope to get there still in one piece. The weather is warm, the sun is shining, it's great sailing right now and within a few days' time we should have forgotten about the heinous Southern Ocean and probably want to do it again." – Stacey

"It has been a long leg and I'm really looking forward to some rest. I think the whole crew are. It's also a little bit of sadness as well, for me this is the best leg of the Volvo Ocean Race, so it's a little bit sad that it's over." – Sam

Itajaí stopover

Coming at the end of the infamous Southern Ocean leg, the three-week stopover in southern Brazil was a welcome relief. It was a relaxed stopover, helped by the laid-back attitude of the local community plus fantastic beaches and clear blue seas.

The public are invited to join a TENA pelvic floor exercise class in front of the SCA Pavilion

Team SCA arrive into Itajaí

A local elderly group are shown the Lego model boat

Team SCA join an initiative to plant indigenous trees in the Parque Natural de Atalaia

Lorena Krueger of Kalmar boatyard presents a wooden kayak, built by Team SCA, to ANI, a local yachting school

InPort guests ready to join Team SCA for racing

Magenta balloons and flags fill the Race Village in anticipation of Team SCA's arrival

A local university orchestra play their way through the Race Village

Public dancing to the beats of Sonia Abreu aka "DJ Grandma"

Colourful messages from fans written on a string of ribbons

DJ Grandma during her set at Magenta Music Night

Sophie (alongside some of the local SCA Pavilion team) imagines life as an elderly person as she tries on the TENA ageing simulator suit

Team SCA racing in the Itajaí ProAm races

Torben Grael joins Team SCA as a guest for the Itajaí InPort Race

Guest Ellen Jabour jumps from Team SCA shortly after the start of Leg 5

A Fight at the Top

Leg 6: Itajaí – Newport

After a good rest from the tough Southern Ocean leg, and a debrief in Brazil, the teams were ready to sail north to Newport in the USA, leaving the Southern Ocean behind them for good. Team SCA were feeling confident and focused for this leg, with conditions the team were familiar with and their thousands of miles of Volvo Ocean Race experience under their belt.

In the first days, the girls enjoyed sailing in the mix with the fleet – close enough to see the other boats' head torches and even smell their food – with plenty of wind-shifts, sail-changes and changing positions between the six boats. On day two, Team SCA was the first boat to tack east, with the rest soon following. The fleet compressed, sticking closely together, with Team SCA in various positions including the lead on day three. On day four, Team SCA tacked north and completed their circumnavigation of the globe, having sailed 36,000 miles since leaving Alicante.

On board, they were feeling proud that they were sailing with the fleet, that they had circumnavigated the planet as part of an all-female team and that they were leading the leg.

Enjoying the warm conditions and fast sailing, there was
frustration on day seven when Team SCA's speed slowed
and they were showing last on the position report. However,
when they reached the doldrums, they were delighted to
be sailing in 15 to 20 knots of breeze and were within
five miles of the fleet.

On day nine, 28 April, there was another milestone to
celebrate as Team SCA were the first boat to cross the equator
back into the northern hemisphere. The next day, leaving the
doldrums, Team SCA hit the tail end of a storm cloud and took
off, with boat speeds of up to 28.5 knots. Warm-water waves
crashed over the cockpit, and the team rotated helms, each
driving the boat just to the edge of control. Conditions were
wet and hot, with relentless waves and saltwater spray so
strong the helms wore goggles. Liz used her surfing skills
to steer the boat along the face of waves.

Sam wrote in the race blog that the team were learning
and improving more than ever, both in teamwork and in
performance – boat speed and strategy. The crew were more
confident, more relaxed, more in tune with the boat and each

other. Although learning from mistakes was frustrating, the crew were keeping the energy positive.

After 17 days and just under 21 hours at sea, they arrived into Newport 12 hours behind the leaders. Sailing better than ever, this was now a crew with a mission. They had spent a week fighting with the leaders – the longest time with the front group – and they liked being there…

Opposite, top:
"This is me and Caroline. It was a hot leg, there is not much wind. This is either early morning or night so it's not that hot. During the night you didn't need a lot of gear on. I wore shorts most of the leg apart from a couple of days out of Newport. When it was really windy we got wet. I remember just wearing shorts and getting wet. You'd only put your gear on to try and let your skin dry off." – Sophie

Opposite, bottom:
"We're setting up a for a sail change so I had to go and transfer a sheet. It's not scary, it's quite fun. You're just swinging around out there, being held on by your harness. You feel like a bit of a monkey."
– Liz

Below:
"We had a really good first week on Leg 6. We crossed the equator just before the other boats but the race was still far from being finished and the last days were a lot harder for us." – Justine

Right:
The fleet encountered a massive patch of sargassum seaweed, which stuck to the bottom of the Team SCA boat, wrapping itself around the keel, the rudder and the propeller shaft and slowing the boat down. The weed needed to be constantly cleared.

"It was four to five days of frustration trying to avoid the seaweed or clear it off the bottom of the boat. It looked so dense that we had to keep trying to convince Sophie that she could not jump off the boat and try to walk over it." – Stacey

Opposite, top:
"Down below you go from white light to red light to preserve your night vision. The hardest thing is going up on deck and waiting for your eyes to adjust, there can be a lot of stumbling around at times."
– Libby

Opposite, bottom, and below:
"My favourite part about sailing at night is the stars. There's no city lights so you can see so many." – Abby

"It's the sheer expanse of the universe above us that has us all in a little bit of awe. There's a whole new world at night. In the sky, there's shooting stars, the moon, the constellations, and in the water the waves glow green."
– Corinna

"My favourite part of sailing at night is the glowing plankton. It's almost as if there's electricity in the sea, so as the waves crash over the bow, the water carries an electric-green colour."
– Justine

Following pages:
"We had three days of really nice weather, flat water and between 15 and 20 knots. It's what we would call 'champagne sailing' – not a cloud in the sky." – Sally

Newport stopover

Newport, Rhode Island, is one of the USA's top sailing centres. Here, family, friends and team supporters visited in their hundreds and Team SCA left a lasting impression on the local community by donating thousands of indigenous saplings.

Tree-planting activity in the SCA Exploration Zone

SCA and WSSCC presenting at the United Nations in New York on "The silence surrounding menstruation for women and girls"

Blogger Nicole Perry takes part in a team fitness session

Girl Scouts join Elodie to help plant trees in Fort Adams State Park

SCA provide pampering for mums on Mother's Day

Guests on board for a ProAm Race

Sam listens to Dongfeng Race Team skipper Charles Caudrelier at the Skippers Press Conference

Girl Scouts proudly sport their new
SCA magenta visors at Fort Adams

Wish of a Lifetime winner Shirley Payne meets Team SCA – (from left to right)
Sophie, Libby, Annie, Shirley Payne and Liz

The Helly Hansen mobile store in the
Race Village

The SCA Pavilion bustling with visitors

ProAm Race guests show off their
first place race medals

Elodie and Corinna visit children at the Pell Elementary
School, Newport

Crowds line the shore at Fort Adams to watch the InPort Race

Captain the dog looks at home on board Team SCA

US blogger Javier Mejia gets pulled up the mast of Team SCA

SO PROUD OF YOU
GO SCA
Go Girls - Go! We're your biggest fans!
Bonjour! Greeting from the Lake of Bienne (Erlach/Neuchâtel) to you in Newport. Abby (Erlach/BE)
CAN IF YOU YOU CAN!
Go Girls Best of luck
Good Luck
Go Girls! Keep it up Joyce
Go SCA!!! Your Amazing -Bethany
WOMAN POWER! So proud, so exciting and so inspiring for all women! Good luck, Best wishes
Great Job Ladies! Will wave to you from our porch
Girl Power! Thx for coming to Newport! And we're your biggest fans so keep it up!
will follow you on instagram!!! -A.J.
Team SCA
You girls Rock!
HEATHER CASEY
You Go Girl!
WAY TO GO GIRLS! WE ARE SO THRILLED YOU'RE HERE. THANKS FOR THE INSPIRATION — BARB + MOE
Enjoy the ride
Inspirational!
Jade Cyrus and Sophia Academy
WONDERFUL EXAMPLE! - NANCY
Stay safe Bring it Home Carol & Joe
GET IT LADIES.
Go girls from the girls
GO GIRLS! PLEASE NO GIRLS OVERBOARD!
You are amazing ladies! So happy to have seen you!
SAIL LIKE A GIRL! SKAL SARA + GRANT
INSPIRED! Megan
Stay Strong
TO SEE AN ALL CHICKS TEAM IN THE MIX!
Awesome Job! You ARE THE BEST!
Girl Power Enjoy your time in Newport
You go girls!
Great job girls! Safe sailing to you all
Go Girls Girl Power!

A Lap of the Planet

Leg 7: Newport – Lisbon

The next leg of the race would take the fleet back across the Atlantic Ocean to Europe in the final dash to Lisbon, Portugal, with the fleet sailing as far north as permitted and, again, watching out for icebergs.

Huge crowds cheered the fleet off for this last ocean leg of the race. It would be the third Atlantic crossing for the boat, the 19th crossing for Dee Caffari and the 21st for Sam Davies, and arriving back to Lisbon would complete the fleet's lap of the planet started in Alicante the previous October.

The fleet set sail in a steady breeze but the wind soon dropped and fog set in. While the other boats were nearby, they could only be seen on the computer screen, and torches were needed to check the trim of the sails.

The choice on this leg for the boats was to take the rhumb line or go south on a longer but possibly faster route. One of the things they could guarantee though was hitching a ride on the Gulf Stream, the powerful Atlantic current that flows from west to east. Team SCA reported small pushes from eddies –

small whirlpools from the Gulf Stream – which meant lots of manoeuvres and adjustments to sail trim.

The fleet was close together, with the first four boats still within a mile of each other on the second day. It was a game of snakes and ladders, with positions constantly changing.

The fleet sailed as far north as possible, right to the bottom of the ice limit. They also passed the area where the ill-fated *Titanic* hit an iceberg and sank in 1912.

As they neared the high pressure of the Azores, Team SCA, who were at the back of the fleet, made a brave move and headed north of the pack, approaching the high pressure 50 miles further north than the rest of the fleet, to try to gain back some lost miles. They were rewarded with stronger winds and faster speeds, and in one day went from being 100 nautical miles behind the leader, to just 17.

They also overtook Abu Dhabi Ocean Racing, but Abu Dhabi Ocean Racing later regained their fifth position and after nine

days at sea, the girls finished in sixth place, just two hours behind them.

Abby said the snakes-and-ladders racing was a world away from where they had been, seven legs before. Now they were right in the detail of how to compete and how to get an extra 0.1 knot of boat speed, while Carolijn was positive that with all their achievements and progress, they were due a good result.

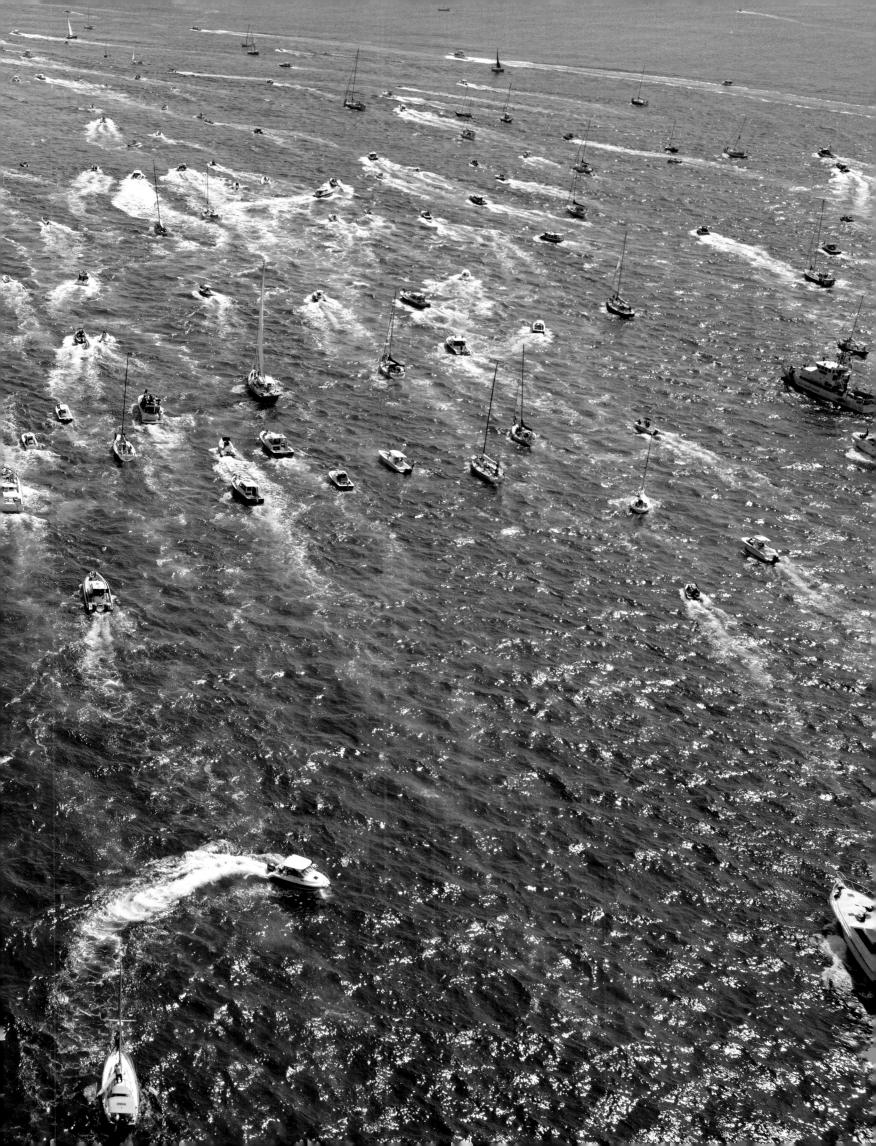

Opposite, top:
"Coming into Lisbon was very fluky. The conditions were changing a lot so we had to constantly move the stack around or fine-tune the sail trim to keep going as fast as we could while looking for the best pressure. It was sunny and flat water so we could take off a few layers – I was coming in off the pole after clearing the furling line." – Liz

We need to put sheets on and off depending on the wind if we're changing sails. This could let go and you'd fall in the water so you're always a bit hesitant. You get used to it. In those conditions, if you did fall you can grab onto a rope and climb back up." – Sophie

Opposite, bottom:
"Blue skies! This was a rare moment without our smock tops on, enjoying the sunshine. Lizzie and I were dropping the A3 and packing it away." – Sara

Below:
"I am putting on a sheet on the Masthead Zero. I am standing on the strops of the outrigger, which is safe enough. I am clipped on to a sheet. Basically it's faster to climb out there without being clipped on.

Previous pages:
"We left Newport in quite light conditions. I am putting an upwind sheet on the Masthead Zero. The wind is shifty, positions are changing all the time, you don't know who'll be the next 'first place' for 10 minutes, so you try to catch every little bit of breeze to move forward."
– Elodie

Opposite, top:
"We just changed sails here to the FRO. This was in the last couple of days, we were heading into the strongest breeze of the leg coming in to Lisbon. We had 18 to 22 knots. By going north we were hoping to have a better angle and to be able to go faster for a longer period and be able to close the gap. Within that we got the maximum boat speed of the leg of 21.7 knots." – Libby

Opposite, bottom, and below:
"The 24-hour blast across from the Azores High to Lisbon was fast, wet and fun. For me there was a twinge of sadness that this was potentially the last time we 'sent it' in strong winds and big waves of an open ocean. I could feel that all the girls had the same sentiment. This was the last time we were unleashing the beast of this boat. We were pushing hard and secretly making sure that we made the most of every minute of this final adrenalin rush."
– Sam

Right:
"We were going through the high pressure at the end of Leg 7. It shows the complexity of timing on that kind of boat, where you often add staysails, use outriggers and can choose where to lead your sheets."
– Justine

Opposite:
Coming into Lisbon in light winds, Liz climbs the mast to spot any wind. Team SCA finished within four hours, 22 minutes and 49 seconds behind the race leader Team Brunel, one of the closest finishes of the race.

Below:
The Team SCA boat being lifted out for routine maintenance in Lisbon, within a couple of hours of the finish. The boats were craned out of the water in all but two ports, so the Team SCA shore team and Volvo Ocean Race Boatyard could check and service the critical areas of the boat and mast.

Lisbon stopover

Once the race arrived back in Europe, the pace of the stopovers picked up.
Team SCA had a packed schedule for the week-long stopover, the highlight of which
was a visit from the team's godmother, Sweden's Crown Princess Victoria.

Young students help with the donation of trees to the city of Lisbon

Liz and Abby celebrate reaching 100,000 Facebook fans with a specially made cake

Bloggers Mariam Hernandez and Phil Gonzalez take in the view

Crown Princess Victoria, Team SCA godmother, with the full sailing squad

Crown Princess Victoria takes the helm at a ProAm Race in Lisbon

Media at a press event with the team at the Team SCA base

Blogger Mariam Hernandez is excited about meeting Team SCA

Graffiti artist 65-year-old Luisa Cortes at work in a Lisbon park as part of an urban art project

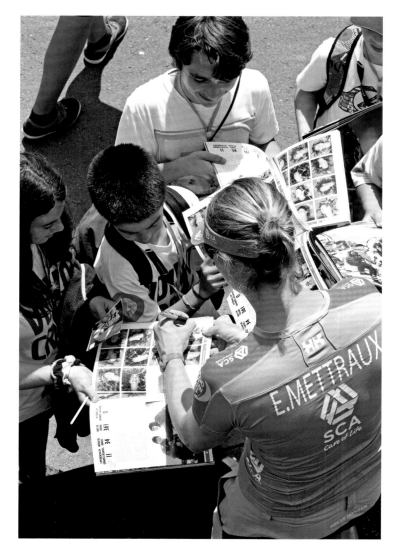

Elodie signs posters for young race fans

Lisbon pavilion hostesses get ready for a busy day

Team SCA fans get ready to cheer the team

161

Sailing to Victory

Leg 8: Lisbon – Lorient

After an exciting week of InPort and ProAm races with blue skies and a scenic backdrop on Lisbon's Tagus River, the fleet left for Lorient, France, on 7 June, making their way north along the Portuguese coast in sun and light winds. The fleet was once again seven boats with the rebuilt Team Vestas Wind rejoining the fleet – it had run aground in the Indian Ocean in Leg 2 and was rebuilt over six months in an Italian shipyard.

As the fleet headed north, fluky winds saw positions changing and then an overnight split in the fleet with a group of four boats offshore to the west and the other three more inshore. After picking up a new breeze, by day two Team SCA had taken the lead and they extended this throughout the day, starting some 5.5 miles ahead of Abu Dhabi Ocean Racing and later positioned 8.1 miles ahead of Team Vestas Wind.

As the fleet tacked up the Portuguese coast, Team SCA stayed close to land as they reached the corner of the coast of Galicia in northwest Spain, still in the lead. The next big milestone would be rounding the iconic Cape Finisterre and

Right:
Abu Dhabi Ocean Racing
and Team SCA sail past
the iconic Cristo Rei statue,
towards the 25 de Abril
Bridge in Lisbon, on the
final inshore section of the
Leg 8 start to Lorient.

then sailing along the Costa da Morte ("Coast of Death"),
so named because of its exposure to the Atlantic Ocean
and its dangerous, rocky shore.

Next came the crossing of the treacherous Bay of Biscay to
Lorient, and by day three Team SCA was bashing upwind
in 30 to 35 knots, with a violent sea state. There were some
bruised and tired crew, with seasickness also taking some
prisoners on the boat, but they were still in first place and
this made any discomfort easier to bear.

When the fleet split again on day three, with three teams
taking a more easterly coastal route, it was nerve-wracking
for Team SCA as they tacked back towards the fleet –
would they cross still ahead of their rivals?

They did, and by 10 June Team SCA had a 10-mile lead
over the rest of the fleet as battles continued behind between
the other boats.

Despite strong winds and violent sea conditions, the team held
their lead. Annie Lush wrote in the race blog that she was

holding her breath on a very happy, but tense boat.

On 11 June, after racing 850 miles, Team SCA crossed the finish line in Lorient in first place to huge cheers as they won Leg 8.

They were the first all-female team to win a leg of the Volvo Ocean Race in 25 years. The team's two and a half years of hard work were finally paying off.

Opposite, top:
"I like driving when it's rough because you feel in control of the boat, you get a feel for what's really happening and how good or bad it is. Sometimes if you're down below or just grinding, you feel unsafe – it might feel worse than it is, but when you get on the helm it's not so bad. It always gives me more confidence, because you're overseeing the whole situation. I really enjoy it. It can be tough and scary but I definitely get a buzz from the adrenalin in those conditions. It's out of control, the waves are big and it's windy but I like that, I like the challenge."
– Sophie

Opposite, bottom:
"First you stack the inside of the boat – the people sleeping down below move the inside stack first, and then everyone comes on deck to stack the sails together. It takes about two and half minutes to move everything across. It's easy if it's light wind, but if the sea state is bad, it takes longer." – Justine

"Stacking in those conditions in the Bay of Biscay is really hard and dangerous, so it needs all of us, but there isn't enough space. We actually made a stacking plan before this leg so we could be as efficient as possible, because it takes four or five of us to lift one sail. Once they are this wet they are more than 100kg each and awkward to manoeuvre with the boat heeled over – and in these conditions, the waves, you can easily lose a sail overboard or crush a person, so we have a team on the windward side, a team in the middle, and a team to leeward, a receiving team. We have a strict method of how we do it." – Annie

Below:
"We're sailing upwind in 30 to 35 knots in big waves, five-metre to six-metre seas, and the boat is bashing up and down on the waves. Generally in these conditions, the biggest accidents happen below deck. Up on deck you're wearing your harness, you're clipped on and you can see a bad wave coming. At night it's harder but you can still see a wave coming. Down below, you lose a bit of perspective of how the boat is moving on the waves, things can happen unexpectedly. Also you need to do things – if you're putting food in a bowl or washing your face, you have to strap yourself with your legs to be able to use your hands. It's tough down below."
– Carolijn

Following pages:
"As soon as we rounded Cape Finisterre, we found ourselves in 35 knots of wind straight down the nose and the waves were really steep. Driving was all about managing the waves and trying not to slam the boat super hard into the back of a wave. It took a lot of effort to manage the boat and drive around the waves. It was freezing cold and the water was cold, I don't think anyone felt very good. You could drive for about an hour or an hour and a half, it was really hard to see, really hard to keep the boat going, so you had to really focus. It was like a permanent ice-cream headache when you were up there. Trimming was the same – we had to rotate trimmers because it was so cold, it gave you a real feeling of this is what this race is really about. That leg we saw all different conditions, and it was a test of keeping the boat going as fast as we could and anticipating what was coming next. We did a really good job of that and having the boat set up right. It made the win really satisfying because we knew we'd sailed through a lot of different conditions." – Sally

Below:
"I love the Brittany coast. I have raced around there and trained around there so much. It's been a long time since I've been there, it was great to bring the boat to what felt like my home port. It's extra special when you come in at night and you know the area, you know the lighthouses, it leaves it to your imagination to remember how the coastline looks, and all the memories come flooding back. It's a special way to come into a place you know, in darkness. It's that extra bit of magic." – Sam

Opposite, top:
Joca, Axel and Brad.

"The coaches finally find their feminine side! This was following through on a promise made to the girls back in Lanzarote that the coaches would be dressed head to toe in pink if we got a podium position on a leg. We didn't want to jinx it by buying them too early. We started talking about it in the morning and we put it off until closing time in the shops that night. There aren't a lot of shops in Lorient that sell that kind of stuff – we were asking for pink blazers and we had some strange looks when we were asking if any of the shops would have pink jackets for three men." – Brad

Opposite, bottom:
"We were really proud to be able to finally give a result back to the team and to the shore crew. We knew we were improving but it was frustrating to not be able to change the position. To be able to finally do that and to be able to come in in first position and hug them was really special. We knew we'd be improving all the race but that wasn't showing in the results so finally to have done it, we proved to everyone that we can do it, and that all the hard work has paid off." – Annie

Following pages:
"It was awesome, we'd won the leg and there was chat about who was going to spray the champagne. All the girls were saying 'you should do it Libby'. The goal was to spray them all, make everyone smell of champagne and enjoy it. Those moments are rare, it's a bit of history to have a leg win." – Libby

Lorient stopover

With Team SCA winning the leg into Lorient, this was a celebratory stopover. The team were mobbed by enthusiastic fans, but perhaps the greatest accolade came from their fellow competitors who gave them a standing ovation at the official prize giving.

Team SCA racing in Lorient's InPort Race

Sam joins a Round Table session with journalists and CEOs

The SCA Kids' Corner exhibition area

Team SCA receive the Leg Winner's trophy at the official prize-giving event in Lorient

A visitor receives special treatment in the Demak'Up skin-care area

Runners taking part in the Color Me Rad event go through the magenta paint arch at kilometre four in Lorient!

Nana Zumba leading one of the daily TENA pilates sessions

Dee and Sara sign posters at a meet-and-greet event at the SCA Pavilion

The Journey Home

Leg 9: Lorient – Gothenburg via The Hague

As the teams left Lorient for the final race leg, Abu Dhabi Ocean Racing had all but sewn up the overall race win, and four teams – Dongfeng Race Team, Team Brunel, Mapfre and Team Alvimedica – were fighting to place second and third overall. For Team SCA, this would be a special journey – they were sailing the boat back to her home port in Sweden, on the final stretch of their 38,739-mile journey around the globe. After their steep learning curve, they were determined to end on a high.

However, the route ahead would be tricky – with strong tides, shipping lanes, wind farms, oil rigs, rocks and multiple exclusion zones to avoid. Right from the Leg Start, the racing was intense, with a gybing duel all the way along the French coast.

At Pointe du Raz on the northwestern tip of France, the fleet split, with Team SCA sticking close to shore and using Sam's local knowledge to get through the tidal gate. The fleet again split at the exclusion zone in the English Channel, with Team SCA staying with the southern group on the French side.

Opposite:
"We were coming in to Raz de Sein and there was a lot of current and not a lot of wind so I was up the mast to try to find the best way to get into the shore and out of the current. We managed to find a good lane into the shore and out of the current for the whole coastline up to the lighthouse. I was up the mast about an hour, while the sun was coming up. I am up there quite a lot. In conditions like this, it's quite peaceful because you can't hear anything so you're in your own little world. In rough conditions it can be bumpy so it can be quite stressful and sometimes painful." – Liz

After a one-day pitstop to The Hague, the fleet started the final 300 miles to Gothenburg. This was the last stretch of the race, possibly the last time the girls would sail together as a team and the last part of their two-and-a-half-year journey. They had taken the SCA message around the world, meeting and inspiring thousands of women and sailors, and creating a huge following. Feelings on board were mixed – they were coming home to friends and family and bringing the boat home, but they were also nearing the end of the race.

After a last close battle with Team Vestas Wind, Team SCA finished in seventh place. Crowds lined the riverside, cheering and waving magenta banners. Sam expressed the emotions of the crew: "We're sad because we feel like now we're at the level where we can be competitive. We just want to keep racing."

But the battle wasn't over yet. There were still podium places in the InPort Race series up for grabs – overall second and third places weren't decided yet and it would all come down to the last race. With an exciting race in light and shifty winds,

Team SCA were second around the first windward mark and they held this place to the finish. This placed them third overall in the InPort Series.

With a leg win, two InPort race wins, and this final InPort podium place, they had finished on a huge high. As Annie said, as the team arrived back to the dock one last time: "It's a brilliant feeling. We wanted everyone to be proud of us – and now they can be."

Previous pages:
"This is Pointe du Raz.
I said to the girls this is
my favourite place in
the world. I said if ever I
did get married, I would
choose to get married on
that point. It took us three
laps to try and get past
it so I think they thought
I was prolonging our
experience!" – Sam

Opposite and below: "This
is the Raz de Sein, one of
the big passages with a
current in Brittany. It can
be really bad when the
weather is not good. Here
it seems like there is wind
but in fact there is no wind,
it's just the current that
makes the waves so you
have four or five knots of
current. Fishing boats that
are often in this area, it's
a special type of fishing,
they are making profit from
the current.

"We had to try three times
to get through and we
were quite lucky to get
through because the tide
had reversed for a while
and we had a really
strong current against us
and no wind. We could
have had to wait two
more hours to get through
if we didn't manage it.
We were the only ones
on this side, the other
boats were on the other
side – they still had a lot of
current and they had to go
around. We won a bit by
going this way." – Justine

Opposite, top:
Crowds line the waterfront in the Race Village at Lorient.

Opposite, bottom:
Carolijn drives Team SCA out of The Hague in the Netherlands where the fleet had a pitstop.

"My house is literally on the shore. When I saw my house, that was a pretty strange feeling, to see your house from the seaside and not have seen it for more than two and a half years. Den Haag itself as a pitstop was amazing. I've never seen anything like it, the enthusiasm and the attention for the sort of sailing in a country like Holland was just mindblowing. It probably hasn't sunk in yet what we've achieved with this race and what it does to people. It's pretty amazing." – Carolijn

Below:
"Even though it was a rainy day, the homecoming was amazing. There were a lot of people all down the river – there were just people everywhere holding SCA flags or with flares and fireworks. It was a very special homecoming, more special because we sail under the Swedish flag. We brought the boat and the team safely back home." – Carolijn

"It was raining and there were hundreds of people with flags. I think it took about an hour to get sorted and it was pouring with rain and they were still standing there with their flags. We'd been waiting for this moment for a long time. It was a pretty long journey and a pretty special end. It was only when we hit the dock and everyone was cheering

and we'd finished the Volvo Ocean Race that I realized, 'oh my goodness, it's over'…" – Annie

"This is that moment. We've done it, we've made it around the world, we're all really happy because we've done what we set out to do. For me as a skipper, your big mission is to bring the boat and the crew home safely, so the weight lifts off your shoulders. We created a really strong bond between all of us. You create a link with everyone that stays for life when you do an experience as intense, with as many highs and lows and challenges, as we've done." – Sam

Gothenburg finish

The Gothenburg stopover, home to SCA, was busy. There was a little sadness that Team SCA, for this race at least, was reaching its conclusion – however, Crown Princess Victoria sailed with the team for the last InPort Race, bringing a fitting royal finale to the sailing.

Icona Pop's Caroline Hjelt braves the top of the mast

Visitors to the SCA Pavilion try the groundbreaking 360-degree film made by the team in the Southern Ocean

Optimist sailors get up close to the Volvo Ocean Race fleet

The fleet jostles for position at the start of the InPort Race

Team SCA receive an ecstatic reception at the SCA office in Mölndal

A bird's-eye view of the Race Village

Team SCA are joined by other winners at the Mange Olsson Foundation presentation

Crown Princess Victoria chats with Annie ahead of the InPort Race

Sophie wins the Hans Horrevoets Rookie Award. The award was presented by his widow and daughters in memory of the Volvo Ocean Race sailor who lost his life in the 2005–06 race

The Team SCA Academy Exhibition in partnership with Getty Images just outside the Gothenburg Opera

Fans have a close view of ProAm racing during the Gothenburg stopover

Team SCA celebrate finishing second in the InPort Race and third overall in the InPort Race series

Former King Juan Carlos of Spain greets the team's godmother Crown Princess Victoria just before she joins the team for the InPort Race

Hilary Lister, the record-breaking quadriplegic sailor, meets Team SCA

Epilogue

It is often only when something comes to an end that there is true understanding of the experience. Team SCA started as an opportunity for women in offshore sailing to show that gender doesn't mean anything. And then, as we stepped off the boat at each stopover, and as the cities were painted magenta, we realized that the Team SCA story was far larger than the race. At every stopover, there were individuals, groups, schools and people of all ages, male and female, with stories to tell of how they had been inspired to go further, to push harder, to start or finish something. To dream. That was moving, humbling and exciting. We realized we were making a difference and that there would be a legacy from all of this, not just in offshore sailing but also across the world in all sorts of ways.

Lining up at the race start in Alicante, against six all-male teams with years of experience, we were an unknown quantity. When we crossed the finish line in Gothenburg nine months later, not just many sea-miles had passed but many life-milestones too, for all of the sailing team, the shore team, the employees of SCA and our countless followers globally.

It was a huge challenge in many ways, from simply existing on the boat, to sailing the boat, to making the boat go faster, and catching up on the experience and knowledge of the other teams. Conditions at times were tough to bear. We all struggled at times. What surprised everyone was how challenging and complex it is to work in such a large team with strong individuals. Everyone had their part to play and flexibility, adaptability and tolerance were required. We were all learning – how to lead, how to make decisions, how to manage expectations. The insight we gained made us stronger and helped us understand and share information. This experience was life-changing and incredibly rewarding. When you succeed as a team, it is unbelievably empowering and one of the greatest rewards out there.

SCA gave us a fantastic opportunity to make a difference. We had a phenomenal amount of support, from our shore team, from our coaches, and people all around the world. They believed that women can compete with men at the elite level of sport and we delivered on this. Now we're champing at the bit to go around that globe again – next time as a boat to be reckoned with.

Libby Greenhalgh
Navigator, Team SCA

Opposite:
The crew of Team SCA (upper level) and the Team SCA shore and commercial teams (ground level).

The Crew

Sally Barkow
Nationality: American
Born: Waukesha, Wisconsin, USA
Hometown: Nashotah, Wisconsin,
USA
Date of Birth: 10 July 1980
Role: Helm/Trimmer and InPort
Race Tactician

Sally has been full-time
sailing since 2002 and prior to
joining Team SCA had been
part of the Olympic sailing
circuit, competing regularly in
offshore regattas in between her
Olympic training programme. Her
career highlights include being
named the Rolex Yachtswoman
of the Year in 2005 and 2007,
and holding the Rolex Women's
Keelboat Champion title for three
years.

Carolijn Brouwer
Nationality: Dutch
Born: Leiden, South Holland, the
Netherlands
Hometown: Leiden, South Holland,
the Netherlands
Date of Birth: 25 July 1973
Role: Watch Captain

Carolijn is an accomplished
multihull and Olympic sailor,
having competed in the Sydney,
Athens and Beijing Games. She
was the only female skipper in
the Tornado multihull class at the
Beijing Olympics. She skippered
the Extreme 40 Holmatro for two
seasons in the Extreme 40 series,
and was at the helm on Amer
Sports Too in the Volvo Ocean
Race in 2001–02.

Dee Caffari
Nationality: British
Born: Watford,
Hertfordshire, United Kingdom
Hometown: Titchfield,
Hampshire, United Kingdom
Date of Birth: 23 January 1973
Role: Helm/Pit

Dee is no stranger to ocean racing
having competed in the Vendée
Globe Race, Global Challenge,
Barcelona World Race and four
transatlantic races. She is the only
woman to have sailed solo around
the world in both directions (east
about and west about) as well
as being the only female to have
sailed around the world three times,
non-stop.

Sophie Ciszek
Nationality: Australian and
American
Born: Mornington, Victoria,
Australia
Hometown: Mornington, Victoria,
Australia
Date of Birth: 28 June 1985
Role: Helm/Bow

Sophie was until 2012 a full-time
crewmember for the Open 60
Hugo Boss. Prior to that she had
a varied career on some of the
world's most renowned racing
yachts, including the Maxis
Wildthing, Brindabella and
Shockwave. Before joining the
project she had sailed more than
60,000 nautical miles – mostly as
bowman – and competed in four
Sydney Hobart Yacht Races.

The full crew of Team SCA: 11 crew and one Onboard Reporter sailed on each leg of the race

Sam Davies
Nationality: British
Born: Portsmouth, Hampshire, United Kingdom
Hometown: Kerlin, Brittany, France
Date of Birth: 23 August 1974
Role: Skipper

Sam is an accomplished single-handed sailor. She has competed in two Vendée Globe Races and has sailed in the challenging Open 60 class for over 10 years. In 2008 she finished the Vendée Globe in fourth place. She was part of the all-female Jules Vernes Trophy attempt in 1998, sailing with Tracy Edwards.

Abby Ehler
Nationality: British and Australian
Born: Plymouth, Devon, United Kingdom
Hometown: Lymington, Hampshire, United Kingdom
Date of Birth: 25 July 1976
Role: Boat Captain/Pit

Abby's entire sailing experience has been in a team environment. She competed in the 2001–02 Volvo Ocean Race with Amer Sports Too. In 2003 she won both the Rolex Fastnet Race and Rolex Middle Sea Race. Abby has a working career in the yachting industry, both on and off the water.

Libby Greenhalgh
Nationality: British
Born: Brighton, East Sussex, United Kingdom
Hometown: Hamble, Hampshire, United Kingdom
Date of Birth: 3 August 1980
Role: Navigator

Prior to joining Team SCA, Libby had been working with the British Sailing Team across Youth, Junior and Olympic levels, providing venue weather forecasts, research support and meteorological education. She has also been a weather forecaster for the Met Office, working both for military forecasting and other sporting events. Libby has vast experience in dinghy sailing, racing an Olympic 470 and an SB20, as well as a variety of 30–35-foot racing boats.

Sara Hastreiter
Nationality: American
Born: South Dakota, USA
Hometown: Wyoming, USA
Date of Birth: 22 September 1984
Role: Bow

Sara had been working towards double-handed offshore racing on Class 40s and other short-handed races as well as campaigning to do a transatlantic before she joined the squad. She had sailed over 40,000 nautical miles and competed in many races, including the Caribbean 600, the Newport to Bermuda Race, IRC Nationals, NYYC Race Week, Antigua Race Week and the St Thomas Rolex Regatta, as well as many deliveries.

Stacey Jackson
Nationality: Australian and British
Born: Mooloolaba,
Queensland, Australia
Hometown:
Mooloolaba, Queensland,
Australia
Date of Birth: 2 June 1983
Role: Bow

Stacey was working as a boat
captain on RP66 Black Jack when
she joined Team SCA. Prior to
that she was a member of a
full-time race crew, RP100. Stacey
has done nine Sydney to Hobart
Yacht Races, with line honours in
2010. She also has multiple wins
in major match racing regattas.
In 2008–09 Stacey worked as
a sailmaker on the shore team
for Telefonica at the India and
Singapore stopovers.

Annie Lush
Nationality: British
Born: Poole, Dorset, United
Kingdom
Hometown: Poole, Dorset, United
Kingdom
Date of Birth: 11 April 1980
Role: Helm/Trimmer

Annie had been racing full time
on the Olympic circuit since
2002 and competed on the
World Match Race Tour, as well
as racing on professional circuits.
She is an Olympic match racer
who competed at the London
Games in the Elliott 6m class and
has been Women's Match Race
Champion three times (2004,
2005, 2010), topping the ISAF
World Ranking in 2010.

Elodie-Jane Mettraux
Nationality: Swiss
Born: Geneva, Switzerland
Hometown: Geneva, Switzerland
Date of Birth: 7 November 1984
Role: Helm/Trimmer

Elodie joined the squad from
Switzerland, where she has a
rich sailing background with
the Geneva Training Centre,
which she has managed for a
number of years. She won the
amateur ranking in the 2012 Tour
de France à la Voile and was
instrumental in building the Swiss
all-female match racing team in
2013. She joined Team SCA as
the fourth under-30 crewmember.

Justine Mettraux
Nationality: Swiss
Born: Geneva, Switzerland
Hometown: Geneva, Switzerland
Date of Birth: 10 April 1986
Role: Helm/Trimmer

Justine joined the team straight
from her Mini-Transat campaign,
spending a year between Team
SCA training and the Mini-
Transat circuit. Justine was a
part of the sailing training centre
in Geneva for 10 years while
competing in many offshore
races, including two Transats, a
Transpacific, and a Tour de France
à la Voile.

Liz Wardley

Nationality: Australian
Born: Kokopo, Papua New Guinea
Hometown: Rabaul, Papua New Guinea
Date of Birth: 6 December 1979
Role: Bow/Helm

Liz is renowned for her numerous titles gained in the Hobie Cat 16 and for her oceanic racing skills. In 1999 she came first overall in the IMS Division 2 of the Rolex Sydney Hobart Yacht Race. The year before, at the age of 19, she was skipper in the Rolex Sydney Hobart Yacht Race. She raced in the Volvo Ocean Race 2001–02 on Amer Sports Too and she has competed many times in the French solo sailing race Solitaire du Figaro.

Anna-Lena Elled

Nationality: Swedish
Born: Borås, Västra Götaland, Sweden
Hometown: Gothenburg, Västra Götaland, Sweden
Date of Birth: 22 April 1975
Role: Onboard Reporter

Anna-Lena is a journalist and the founding editor of *Search Magazine*, a sailing magazine in Sweden. She is a keen sailor, sailing her F18 catamaran off the west coast of Sweden, and also enjoys taking part in other extreme sports. She was introduced to the team by Magnus Olsson, who recommended her for the role of Onboard Reporter.

Corinna Halloran

Nationality: American
Born: Newport, Rhode Island, USA
Hometown: Newport, Rhode Island, USA
Date of Birth: 25 August 1985
Role: Onboard Reporter

Corinna grew up with a camera in her hand and went on to study photojournalism and writing at the University of San Francisco, and she has a professional certificate in Visual Storytelling awarded by Maine Media College. She has a passion for the ocean and sailing and has worked in the super yacht industry and on boats extensively for several years.

Volvo Ocean Race 2014-15

THE VOLVO OCEAN 65

Hull Length	(ISO 8666) 20.37m (66ft)
Hull Beam overall (ISO 8666)	5.60m (18.4ft)
Max Draft (Keel on CL)	4.78m (15.8ft)
Boat Weight (empty)	12,500kg (27,557lb)
Keel arrangement	Canting keel
Daggerboards	Twin fwd daggerboards
Rudders	Twin fixed rudders
Rig Height	30.30m (99.4ft)
Bowsprit Length	2.14m (7ft)
Mainsail Area	163m²
Working Jib Area	133m²
Upwind Sail Area	468m² (mainsail and masthead Code 0) 296m² (mainsail and working jib)
Working Jib Area	578m² (mainsail and A3)

Results – Races Overall	Leg 1	Leg 2	Leg 3	Leg 4	Leg 5	Leg 6	Leg 7	Leg 8	Leg 9	Total
1 Abu Dhabi Ocean Racing	1	3	2	2	1	2	5	3	5	24
2 Team Brunel	3	1	5	5	4	3	1	5	2	29
3 Dongfeng Race Team	2	2	1	3	8	1	4	7	4	33
4 Mapfre	7	4	4	1	2	4	2	4	3	34
5 Team Alvimedica	5	4	3	4	3	5	3	6	1	34
6 Team SCA	6	6	6	6	5	6	6	1	7	51
7 Team Vestas Wind	4	8	8	8	8	8	8	2	6	60

Results – InPort Series	Alicante	Cape Town	Abu Dhabi	Sanya	Auckland	Itajaí	Newport	Lisbon	Lorient	Gothenburg	Total
1 Abu Dhabi Ocean Racing	2	1	3	2	6	2	3	2	4	6	31
2 Team Brunel	4	2	2	4	2	1	5	5	6	1	32
3 Team SCA	6	3	1	5	1	4	4	4	5	2	35
4 Mapfre	3	7	6	6	3	5	1	1	2	3	37
5 Team Alvimedica	1	6	5	3	5	6	2	3	1	5	37
6 Dongfeng Race Team	5	4	4	1	4	3	6	6	3	4	40
7 Team Vestas Wind	7	5	8	8	8	8	8	7	7	7	73

DID NOT START: 8 points   DID NOT FINISH: 8 points   RETIRED: 8 points   GIVEN REDRESS: Decided by the Jury

RACES OVERALL AND INPORT SERIES: Each team gets the same points as their finishing position – for example, first place gets 1 point. All legs count and lowest score overall wins. InPort Race results are only used in the event of a tie in the overall Race.

Credits

THE AUTHOR

Yvonne Gordon is an award-winning features writer and broadcaster whose work has been in publications around the world. She is also an experienced sailor, has won a number of local dinghy titles, and has competed at European and World Championship level in dinghies and sportsboats. Yvonne also writes travel books and she has sailed to remote island archipelagos around the world including in Norway, Cuba and Burma.

THE PHOTOGRAPHERS

Anna-Lena Elled, an Onboard Reporter with Team SCA, is also a journalist and the founding editor of *Search Magazine*, a sailing magazine in Sweden. She is a keen sailor, sailing her F18 catamaran off the west coast of Sweden, and she also enjoys taking part in other extreme sports.

Corinna Halloran, an Onboard Reporter with Team SCA, grew up with a camera in her hand and went on to study photojournalism and writing at the University of San Francisco. She has a professional certificate in Visual Storytelling awarded by Maine Media College. She has a passion for the ocean and sailing and has worked in the super yacht industry and on boats extensively for several years.

Rick Tomlinson is an internationally recognized yachting photographer. He raced in the Whitbread Round the World Race on board Drum, The Card, Intrum Justitia and Team EF. For the Volvo Ocean Race, he has twice worked as the Official Race Photographer and twice as a Team Photographer. Based in Cowes, Isle of Wight, Rick travels the world on assignments for sailing events, magazines and yacht builders.

We are grateful to the following photographers for their contributions to this book:

Anna-Lena Elled – Team SCA
Corinna Halloran – Team SCA
Rick Tomlinson – Team SCA
Raquel Clausi – Team SCA Academy (Alicante)
Alecsandra Raluca Dragoi – Team SCA Academy (Cape Town)
Jessica Pepper-Peterson – Team SCA Academy (Abu Dhabi)
Ana Caroline da Lima – Team SCA Academy (Sanya)
Zelda Gardner – Team SCA Academy (Auckland)
Ellen Wissink – Team SCA Academy (Itajaí)
Sara Strandlund – Team SCA Academy (Newport and Gothenburg)
Teo Jioshvili – Team SCA Academy (Lisbon)
Holly Powers – Team SCA Academy (Gothenburg)
Pedro Martínez – Martínez Studio
Bárbara Sánchez – Martínez Studio
Ainhoa Sanchez – Volvo Ocean Race
Ricardo Pinto – Volvo Ocean Race
Brian Carlin – Team Vestas Wind
Yann Riou – Dongfeng Race Team
James Tomlinson – Rick Tomlinson Photography

Captions for the preliminary pages

Page 2: Team SCA in the Round Britain and Ireland Race
Page 4: The full Team SCA squad
Page 7: Team SCA on sea trials in the English Channel a few days after launching in the UK

© Bokförlaget Max Ström, 2015
This book has been produced by Max Ström on behalf of Team SCA, to celebrate SCA's all-female team in the Volvo Ocean Race 2014–2015.

Text: Yvonne Gordon with Team SCA
Picture Editor: Rick Tomlinson
Design: Osborne Ross Design, London
Editorial directors: Victoria Low and Jeppe Wikström
Editor: Christopher Westhorp
Book Steering Group: Gabriella Ekelund and Richard Brisius
With special thanks to Joséphine Edwall-Björklund,
Gordana Landén and Christoph Michalski
Repro: Linjepunkt, Falun, Sweden
Printed by: Graphicom, Italy, 2015

ISBN: 978-91-7126-346-9

For further information on SCA and Team SCA please visit:
www.sca.com and
www.teamsca.com

The *No Ordinary Women* documentary series about Team SCA preparing for the Volvo Ocean Race can be viewed on the SCA YouTube channel:
youtube/SCAeveryday

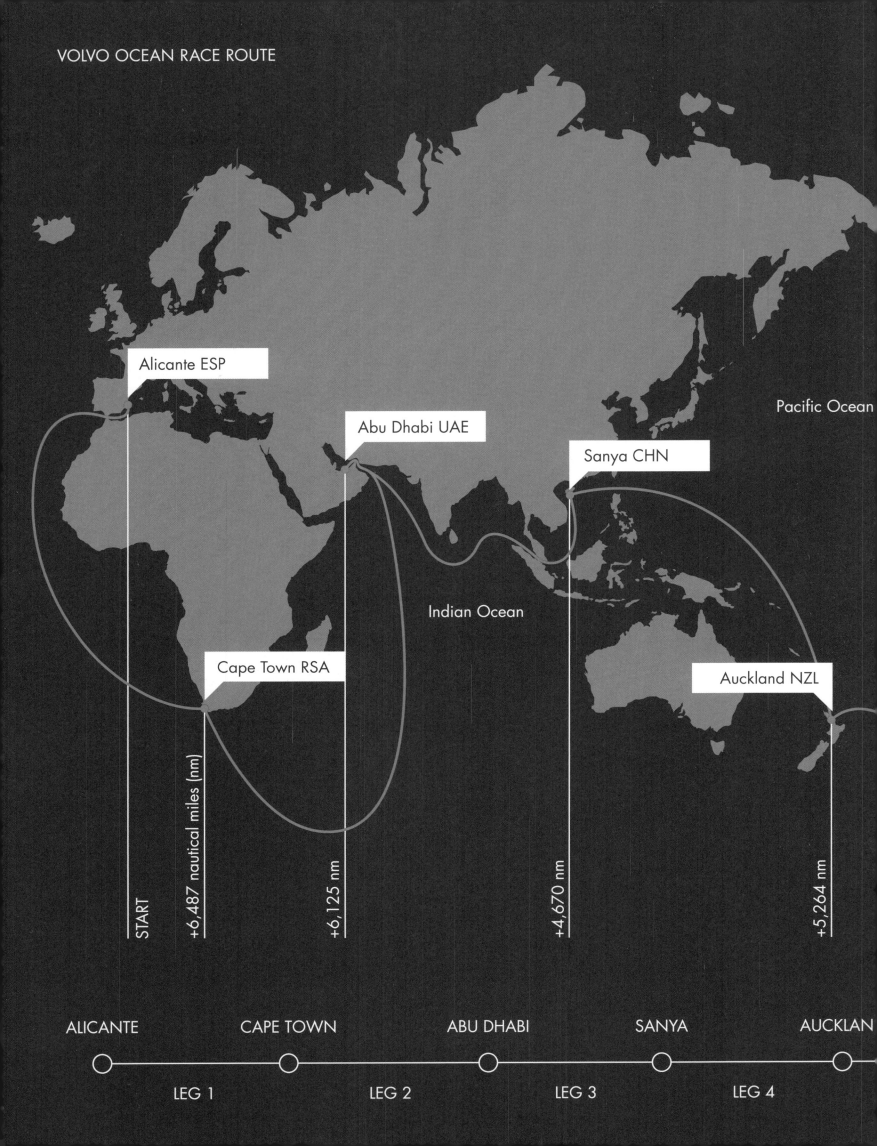